RAMESH CHANDRA AGARWAL

RAMESH CHANDRA AGARWAL

The man who created the Dainik Bhaskar Group

BHARATHI S PRADHAN

AMARYLLIS

AMARYLLIS
An imprint of Manjul Publishing House Pvt. Ltd.
•7/32, Ansari Road, Daryaganj, New Delhi 110 002
Website: www.manjulindia.com
Registered Office:
•10, Nishat Colony, Bhopal 462 003 – India

This edition first published in 2019

ISBN 978-93-89647-04-4

Printed and bound in India by Thomson Press (India) Ltd.

We acknowledge the contribution of Prakash Biyani

CONTENTS

FOREWORD BY
SADHGURU

This biography of Ramesh Chandra Agarwal by Bharathi Pradhan is an interesting and frank narrative of the life and work of a person who had a tremendous impact on the fourth estate of the Indian democracy. It offers an intimate ring-side view of the mild-mannered man whose steely resolve and extraordinary business acumen changed the face of regional language news in this country.

At a time when this nation was still lumbering under the colonial cross of double standards for English language and regional language news publications, this man boldly subverted the dominant paradigm, and for this we owe him credit and admiration.

In my personal interactions, I saw a gentle but astute man and mind. One cannot help admiring the spirit of adventure and tremendous dedication with which he approached all aspects of his work.

This retelling of his life will certainly inspire many others.

Much Regard & Blessings
Sg

FOREWORD BY SADHGURU

INTRODUCTION

THE MAN, THE PUBLISHER

In 2017, Steven Spielberg made a true to life film called *The Post* with Meryl Streep and Tom Hanks. *The Washington Post* was a local paper in the 1970s, when President Nixon's government knew that they were losing the war in Vietnam but lied consistently to the American people even as thousands of young boys continued to be drafted and sent to fight only to return in coffins. The secret Pentagon Papers had it all, they had the whole sordid documented proof.

When the indomitable investigative editorial team of *The Washington Post* used its connections and got hold of it, the decision to take on their friends in the administration and publish the Pentagon Papers, was the toughest call Katherine Graham, the first female publisher in the US (Streep), and editor Ben Bradlee (Hanks) had to take in their careers. But that one decision turned *The Washington Post* from a local paper to what it is today.

The Pentagon Papers happened to *The Washington Post* in the 70s in America.

A similar story happened in 1984 in the eastern part of the globe—to *Dainik Bhaskar* in Bhopal, India.

'Opportunities are like sunrises. If you wait too long, you miss them,' said William Arthur Ward.

Opportunity came in the form of courage shown in the aftermath of an epic tragedy.

On the night of 2 December 1984, there were two human stories running parallel in Bhopal. One was that of the unsuspecting sleeper upon whom the icy fingers of death stealthily crept.

The other was that of the unflagging entrepreneur who embarked to tell the story of the sleeper in all its stark, naked truth.

This is the saga of that entrepreneur.

Ramesh Chandra Agarwal, the undaunted newspaper man who glimpsed an opening to make culpable authorities accountable, went to work. He grabbed the opportunity, and in the process built a strong company profile—of fearless journalism that tells the story as it is.

And Ramesh Chandra took his first step towards establishing *Dainik Bhaskar* as the No. 1 newspaper of India.

A NOTE FROM THE AUTHOR

Facts and figures, personal tales and professional episodes, and all such material required to bring alive the riveting life of Mr Ramesh Chandra Agarwal were supplied and vetted by his worthy sons Sudhir, Girish and Pawan.

Additionally, they provided me with an English translation of Prakash Biyani's biography on the media baron for me to use as background material.

They also arranged meetings with a smorgasbord of political leaders, associates and business strategists whose invaluable inputs contributed to building this story of leonine courage and leadership that was wrapped with surprising humility.

A book without a publisher would be like a master chef without a kitchen. Vikas Rakheja, Rashmi Menon and Manoj Kulkarni of Amaryllis gave *Anant…* the warm editorial support that every author cherishes.

To all who helped me recreate the life of a people's man extraordinaire, *dhanyavaad*!

Bharathi S Pradhan

Chapter 1

GENESIS & GENES

'You can't go back and change the beginning.
But you can start where you are and change the ending'

– CS Lewis

Two lives.

Both demanding and on par: equal status, equal importance, clamouring for equal ardour. In an impossible grand opera.

Both centrepieces of a single life, neither a sub-text of the other.

Both tracks he deftly juggled and merged without acrimony, in fact, with symphonic harmony – two tunes segueing into a majestic composition.

Indeed, how Ramesh Chandra Agarwal led both his lives with such distinguished success will always remain one of the finest lessons in polyphony or the synthesising of a number of parts.

Ramesh Chandra Agarwal's two consummate ecstasies that

would have tired out a lesser man were: first, as a man born to business who dared strike out on his own and risk it all, again and again, to build an empire with a turnover of Rs 5,000 crore in a period of 35 years.

His equally important other was as the patriarch who devoted his life to nurturing a growing family, inclusive in its acceptance of diversity, willing to embrace change, to finally stand triumphantly united as the bastion of the joint family system.

The world watched, he performed.

Agarwal Bhawan, Sultaniya Road, Ibrahimpura, Old City, Bhopal

Circa 1980

During a significant phase of his life, Ramesh Chandra Agarwal had something in common with the President of the United States: his house was above his workplace.

With the clatter of printing machines downstairs and the chatter of a robust family one flight above and in rooms on the terrace, the boundary lines blurred blissfully. To the outsider who didn't get an inner view, the points of contact seemed to merge harmoniously.

What the eye outside Agarwal Bhawan captured was the warmth of a Vaish Marwari family with three generations bound together by blood and business.

On a typical day, Pawan, not yet ten years of age, would throw his school bag and dash to the dispatch department to extract postage stamps from a pile of letters and packets.

An essentially happy child, Ramesh Chandra's third son would take two steps at a time and run up to add the new additions to his precious stamp collection. Pawan couldn't be bothered about what transpired downstairs. His father, two older brothers, his grandfather, uncles and older cousins, were all involved in the business of bringing out a daily newspaper and a press that rolled out notebooks for schools.

His sister Bhawna, younger by three years and his only female sibling, was untouched by the business too, although she would also stray down occasionally to help fold the copies of their family-owned newspaper, glue pages or pass on a letter or two.

Veritably, Pawan's older brothers, Sudhir and Girish, were already the hands-on guys, familiar with the workings of their modest legacy: *Dainik Bhaskar*, the newspaper which did reasonably well in Bhopal, a growing city in Madhya Pradesh, India.

It was only father Ramesh Chandra Agarwal who watched the hum of harmony between upstairs and downstairs with his heart doing an arrhythmic beat. His life, he knew deep down, would have to take a turn where he would have to bid goodbye to his past and march into a new, uncharted future.

But right now, it was 9 pm and he had to call up his father in Gwalior to file his daily report.

Ramesh Chandra's father, Dwarka Prasad Agarwal, the impressively dominating patriarch of the family, had migrated southward from Jhansi in Uttar Pradesh to Bhopal in the neighbouring state of Madhya Pradesh, later summoning his younger brother Vishambhar Dayal who brought his family with him. His youngest sibling Mahesh Prasad remained in Jhansi. Business coursed naturally in a Marwari's veins and working together as a family was an instinctive herd characteristic of the community.

Dwarka Prasad and wife Kasturi Devi had one son—Ramesh Chandra was born in Jhansi on 30 November 1944.

The father and son were like two contrasting sets of suits cut from the same cloth.

One seemed tailored to be aggressive, fussy, fastidious; particular, picky, pernickety; stylish and short-tempered. A stand-out, larger-than-life presence whose arrival always seemed to send the household into a tizzy.

The other, fashioned more subtly, was uncritical and undemanding; unassuming, understated; pleasant, placid, equable and humble. You wouldn't even know he was home.

But both men knew no word that spelt fear. They were two men endowed with entrepreneurial skills and a flair for networking long before the word became fashionable, each blessed with a business brain in which was imbedded a calculator. A father-son team in which each stood his ground with firm determination in a face-off.

Cut from the same cloth, a clash was waiting to happen.

To fully comprehend the two main dramatis personae of the opening sequence, the rise of Dwarka Prasad Agarwal the trenchant businessman from Jhansi, needed to be documented.

A man of medium height of about 5′7″, he was fair-skinned with black hair that he didn't dye to his dying day. Peering through sharp, keen eyes that seldom required spectacles, he seemed much taller. Robust and razor-sharp, potent and powerful, he could put the fear of the devil in those around him. He wore his spotless dhoti-kurta without a turban but with stand-out pride.

In the early 1950s, when Dwarka Prasad shifted to Bhopal, he lived in a rented house and established the Bhopal Stationery Mart where he sold paper, notebooks and stationery, and published notebooks for schools after winning a tender for it from the government.

For four years, he also edited and published a four-page Hindi newspaper named *Prakash* (meaning, light) and with that he got his first taste of the respect and reach of the media. In 1958, he moved from a 'light' name to the luminescence of the glorious sun when he got the *Bhaskar* title.

Printed on a treadle machine, Dwarka Prasad's daily newspaper with the blazing logo of *Dainik Bhaskar,* which would translate into 'The Daily Sun', was born in August 1958.

With business expansion came his office-cum-residence in Ibrahimpura and Shaukat Mahal, a building he soon bought in the same neighbourhood. In his lifetime, Dwarka Prasad established multiple firms in Bhopal including DP Agarwal & Brothers, Noble Paper Corporation and Bharat Paper Mart. He was also the dealer for Ballarpur Paper Mill and Shrigopal Paper Mill. His status as a newspaperman gave Dwarka Prasad access to men of great influence and firm friendships were forged between him and eminent politicians including Congress leaders and Chief Ministers of Madhya Pradesh like Dwarka Prasad Mishra, Arjun Singh, Prakash Chandra Sethi and Govind Narayan Singh.

His son Ramesh Chandra, taller than his father by a couple of inches, was barely 15 years old when Dwarka Prasad drew him into the family business. Starting from the shop floor in the dispatch department of *Dainik Bhaskar* (DB) where he bundled and tied the paper and took it to the market, Ramesh Chandra got speedily acquainted with the entire process of bringing out a newspaper and even more importantly, of selling it. It was irreplaceable hands-on experience as he got his first exposure to what would become one of his chief assets as a media baron—of establishing a splendid communication with hawkers who were a vital cog in the delivery machinery that took the paper to its readers in the pre-digital era.

Ramesh Chandra also got an early feel of how to deal with disappointments when he launched two newspapers that had to be aborted almost on take-off—*Aftaab-e-Jadeed* in Urdu and *National Mail* in English. The two failures toughened him for a future where ups and downs had to be handled with equanimity, and they readied him to come back energised after every setback.

"All of us lived in Ibrahimpura, in the house that my

grandfather built in 1958, until the business started expanding, the family grew and my uncle Vishambharji moved to another house about a kilometre away," recalled Ramesh Chandra's second son, Girish.

Comic chaos ruled inside Agarwal Bhawan. 'Bhabhi' is the Hindi term used to address an older brother's wife while the father's older brother is called 'Tauji'. Dwarka Prasad's brothers called him Bhaiya (older brother) and his wife Kasturi Devi was their Bhabhi. The brothers' children called their uncle and aunty Tauji and Taiji. Which was all as per the rule book.

But when Ramesh Chandra grew up hearing his young uncles (who were hardly older than him) call his father Bhaiya and his mother Bhabhi, he and his two sisters too picked up the habit. His father thus became Bhaiya (not Papa) and his mother became Bhabhi (not Ma).

Similarly, because Dwarka Prasad's nephews called him Tauji and his wife Taiji, his grandchildren (Ramesh Chandra's brood of four) also addressed them the same way and not as Dada (grandfather) and Dadi (grandmother).

That's what happened in joint families of yore where the age gap between siblings would sometimes be more than that of a parent and offspring. Therefore, cousins and uncles would often belong to the same age bracket.

It took a while to figure out these simple complications but once understood, the dynamics of dynasty, drama and daring could move on.

With time, there emerged three clash points that created a schism between father and son to the extent where they would one day be hiring lawyers against each other in a courtroom confrontation.

One of the areas of incompatibility was the obvious, overt dissimilarity in their personalities.

Under the surface too, there simmered differences. They

contrasted in the way they wanted to conduct the family business. Dwarka Prasad was essentially a businessman; Ramesh Chandra, an empire builder. A businessman balanced his ledger at the end of the day to stay in profit; an empire builder had his vision on the future. For him, the day's figures were immaterial.

"My grandfather was terrifyingly aggressive," stated Sudhir, "while my father took after his mother and was very docile.

"Dadaji was a very stylish man, rather fixed about his likes and dislikes. He would travel only first class in trains even in those days. He would use only Pears soap and a particular brand of cream. He would eat only certain foods that had to be prepared and served in a particular way. With his tea, he had to be served two slices of bread of only a specific brand and Amul butter, no other, with freshly sliced tomatoes that had to be cut only five minutes before serving. Any departure from these instructions and he wouldn't touch it. Or worse, he would just throw it. He was rigid, tough and unbending."

But it was his grandfather who introduced Sudhir to the newspaper business and gave him thorough, hands-on training.

He described the work culture under his grandfather. "I started working when I was barely 12½ years old and I remember my grandfather being very strict with everybody. In the Ibrahimpura setup, it was an open office culture with no cabins. There was a large hall with one big table where my grandfather would sit. All the staff would sit in front of him or to his left. We lived upstairs in the same building. When I'd come back from school around 4 o'clock, my grandfather's mandate for me was to be down at 6 pm and sit in the office for two hours every day.

"I was in Class 7 or 8 when he started me off like a peon. '*Upar se chai lekar aayiye*, please go and fetch tea from upstairs,' or go and give some paper to somebody or go bring something from that person. I was essentially the go-fetch, errand boy. He then put me in charge of petty cash. He would give me Rs 200 which was kept in a small box. Out of that I would pay 1 or 2 rupees for tea and other sundry items and keep track of the expenses. After a while, he made me the official storekeeper of the company for items like inks and plates. I'd come back from school, run and open the store, and release the material.

"But an even earlier memory I have is of a huge fight between my father and my grandfather around 1975-76 when I was still too young to comprehend it completely. For the first time, I saw my father stand up and firmly take on my grandfather. There was a place called Shahdol in MP where we had a newspaper called *Dainik Janbodh*. I don't know who started it or why it was started but somebody was running it for my grandfather. After this fight, my father left home, went over to my uncle, Vishambharji's printing unit and asked him for a place in his godown to stay in as an interim arrangement.

"I was a kid but I remember my father putting us in his jeep early in the morning and taking us to the godown where we, oblivious to the seriousness of the situation, settled down within minutes and started playing.

"My father told his father that he would take his mother and his family and go to Shahdol to take care of the other paper. We ended up living in that godown for more than 30 days.

"Mummy was pregnant with my sister Bhawna, when we lived in a portion of the godown. She would cook in a corner and we'd sleep in that temporary makeshift home while my father worked with Vishambharji in his office for some time. We didn't go to Shahdol ultimately as my father and grandfather reached an understanding and we were soon back in Agarwal Bhavan."

"Yes, my father and my grandfather were indeed poles apart," Girish drew the differences verbally.

Ramesh Chandra's second son had a schoolboy's fascination for the patriarch who terrified everybody around him. And, in the Agarwal family, it was noted with much amusement that Girish was the one who seemed most inclined to take after his imperialistic grandfather.

Nodding with a chuckle, Girish said, "From what I remember of my early days, my father had a calm, docile, subdued, almost non-existent identity while my grandfather was fiery, fearsome, hot-headed and a very angry man. Landing a few slaps on someone's face was common, par for the course with him.

"I was totally in awe of my grandfather's intimidating personality," he candidly admitted. "I idolised him. Whenever he visited us, I'd ensure that I had my lunch with him because he had to be served a proper thali (traditional plate) with pickles, salad, dal, *sabziyan* (vegetables), roti, everything in its right place and cooked to perfection. When he wasn't around, we'd get food in a normal plate and I wanted to be stylish like my grandfather.

"I loved the whole atmosphere that prevailed in the house, everybody going into a tizzy tension because grandfather was coming over. On the other hand, I never saw anybody at home working up a lather that Papa was scheduled to arrive any moment. But when Dadaji was on his way, the whole household was on its toes to keep things spic and span and ready for him."

Ramesh Chandra was different from Dwarka Prasad in temperament but when he saw bits of his father in Girish, he indulged him.

"Papa would joke that I was their Bombay Dyeing *beta* (son) because I was so brand conscious. Like my grandfather, I too didn't like normal bed linen but loved fresh white Bombay Dyeing sheets.

"I would subconsciously compare my father with my grandfather. I was Dadaji's favourite kid, I could go to him with any demand and be sure that he'd fulfil it. In fact, when everybody else ignored me, I would wait for Dadaji to come, so I could ask for a new shirt or anything else. And he'd say, *chalo*, come on, and take us to the market. The only thing was, he'd take everybody along, so everybody else also got a new shirt."

The change in Ramesh Chandra Agarwal happened gradually and it was only a matter of time before his sons began to admire the emergence of a more assertive personality in their father.

"As he became more involved with the business, I saw my father change," recorded Girish. "He was so hardworking, he'd work late into the night, come home, wake up in the middle of the night and go back to the office again. What is etched in my memory is how particular my father and my grandfather were about the daily 9 pm reporting system."

Ramesh Chandra who didn't fuss over wardrobe, food or mode of travel, had however, one major weakness: he was a movie buff, an inveterate cinema-goer who watched every film that was released in his city. It was a family outing as he'd gather whoever was free and take off to the cinema hall. But even though he loved the movies, his children remembered that they would often miss the beginning as they would reach the hall 15-20 minutes after the film had started. This was because the 9 pm report to his father was sacrosanct. Those were days when even STD (Subscriber Trunk Dialling) was not available on domestic phone lines. Ramesh Chandra had to therefore book a trunk call to wherever his father was and give him a detailed report on the activities of the day.

"Dadaji was very, very sharp and had a natural flair for numbers," stated Sudhir. "If you wrote a number on a piece of paper and showed it to him, it would remain etched in his mind. So, in that mandatory 9 pm call, if my father mentioned a wrong figure, my grandfather would jump at him and say, '*Tum galat bol rahe ho.* You're wrong.' My father had to therefore make sure he always got the figures right before he spoke to his father. This affinity for figures was handed from my grandfather to my father and from him to me."

But the emergence of fault lines in the family were not too far away.

Dwarka Prasad had foreseen the problems that would plague the business and had done an informal division earlier in the 1970s where he and his brother handled the business of printing books and stationery that were supplied to the government and job orders for printing while the considerably smaller business of DB was handed over to Ramesh Chandra.

"Initially it was, we do the printing business, you run the paper," Girish put it in perspective. "But once the paper became successful, everybody wanted a piece of the pie and that became a major issue.

"In the early 1970s, the Gwalior edition of *Bhaskar* was established. But when there was a split in the early 80s, my grandfather continued with the business in Gwalior while we continued with ours."

Although Girish had all along preferred his grandfather's authoritarian imperiousness over his father's seeming meekness, once Ramesh Chandra took his stance in the ring, his family became his cheerleaders.

"When he started off on his own in 1981, he was sure of how he wanted to run the show as head of the family. And I began to see signs of aggression in him," noted Girish with approval.

"Once, when I had gone to see him off at the airport, one of the security guards stopped me and didn't let me go inside. When my father asked him, 'Why have you stopped my son?,' the security person said that I didn't have the requisite permission for entry. My father didn't take it lying down and demanded, 'I just saw two or three *netas* (political leaders) walk in, what about them?'"

Girish was bemused and impressed. "I found it very unusual that my father was fighting for me. I thought, wow, he can get angry too," laughed Girish. "Publicly, I'd never seen my father get furious with anybody."

At home, he had seen glimpses of it. "I once got a *thappad,* a tight slap, from my father when we were up to some mischief in the old house. I was sliding down the banisters and he saw that I could have slipped and hurt myself. It worried him. So he gave me one tight slap across the cheek. I think this was around the time Gudiya (sister Bhawna) was born. Until then, I'd never seen that side of him."

Though they were at daggers drawn over a personal issue, Dwarka Prasad began to see flashes of himself in his son. He saw the fearlessness, the readiness to take risks, and the stubbornness too. He was perceptive and when he sized up his son's capabilities, he realised with pride that Ramesh Chandra was a natural businessman.

But Dwarka Prasad's anger issues remained unchanged. Ramesh Chandra's only daughter Bhawna may have been a kid but she knew enough to remark, "When Mummy got married, my grandfather was boundlessly strict. Papa knew it would be tough going for her, so he had told my mother that she would have to manage her father-in-law's anger because he wasn't going to change his ways.

Through the vile bouts of temper and the vagaries of life and business, what made Ramesh Chandra stronger and more successful by the day was the unwavering and resolute support he received from his wife, Sharda Devi.

It wasn't easy for the educated Sharda Devi who had gone to college and held a degree, to adjust to life in a family where crotchety unpredictability ruled. It was also a household where even basic requirements were missing when she went in. Her mother-in-law Kasturi Devi was someone who'd led a tough life from her early days and had grown up without supervised grooming.

Bhawna elaborated, "My Dadi (i.e. Ramesh Chandra's mother) got married when she was only 12 years old and she'd lost her mother very early in life. She often told me that she was such a kid that when her mother's funeral bier was leaving the house, she danced her way through it without an inkling of how somber the occasion was. She didn't even realise that she had lost her mother forever. Nobody was around to teach the motherless girl to even have nice crockery in the house. So when my mother stepped into the family, she told my father that she wanted good crockery and he bought it for her from Bombay (as the city was then called). Papa would say that Mummy had a fondness for sarees but in a joint family, if you bought something, it had to be for everyone. So he'd stop himself from buying her anything. He didn't remember ever buying her jewellery either because of this practice. But my father always talked about how well Mummy adjusted to her new house uncomplainingly. Even when Papa had the fight with my grandfather and left the house, she didn't question him on how they would manage in a small garage. He told us, 'Without any help from me, she set up the kitchen in one corner. I would give her only Rs 500 for the month and she not only managed splendidly, she would even squirrel away a little from it and help me out with the savings she had put away.'"

Ramesh Chandra began to show new levels of maturity after he shifted out of the house his father had built and struck out a path of his own. The first independent step he took was to shift out of Agarwal Bhawan and move into a large, rented bungalow in the upscale Arera Colony of Bhopal with his wife and children. The next was to build his own sprawling mansion in the same plush residential area. Ramesh Chandra became the head of his independent nuclear family and underwent a personality switch in his new role.

His sister Meena revealed more on her brother and her father, two different men who were bound by blood and some similar traits.

For all his cantankerous ways, Dwarka Prasad was also an

admirable man who had sown the seeds of enterprise in his family and had done it with uncompromising toughness. Vaish families traditionally controlled the input cost of their businesses to register a heftier profit. In his younger days in Jhansi, Dwarka Prasad was known to go to Allahabad to buy books and carry bundles of them back on his shoulders to save the cost of paying coolies.

It was again a Vaish thought that only sons would carry on the family business and they didn't need formal education for it—they believed that there was nothing in schoolbooks that could replace on-site experience. If Dwarka Prasad sent his son Ramesh to school it was solely to gain proficiency in mathematics, to do sums in the head without using pen and paper.

Born in 1948, Meena Garg was four years younger than Ramesh Chandra, the brother she referred to as Bhaisaab all her life. 12 years junior to Meena was Neelam Goyal, the youngest of the siblings, who is now based in Mumbai.

Old enough to remember and close enough to her brother to understand him, Meena portrayed the family she was born into, in her own simple way.

"My father was never in favour of us studying, he always felt, what's the use of an education? He would actually distribute *laddoos* (sweets) if one of us failed in class," she gave a half-smile. "He'd say, 'Good, you can spend one more year in that class.'

"All of us were petrified of him, terrified of even uttering a word in his presence," she said with a shiver. "If at night he said it was day, we would nod and agree. We were that scared of him. Since I was the older daughter, I was quite his favourite and whenever he had to meet someone or had some work to do, he would take me along. He believed that I was his lucky charm.

"Although nobody could speak up before him, my brother would often come up with some excellent suggestions. Initially, they were in the business of printing notebooks for schools that were based on orders they procured from the government. They were printing books for children up to Class 3 when Bhaisaab suggested, 'Why don't we start printing for Class 4 too? It'll be good for us to keep moving forward and to progress.' But my father ruled it out sharply saying, 'We can barely manage the Class 3 books, how are we going to handle any more?' My brother, however, persisted and said, 'Let us attempt this in bits? Maybe print only the Mathematics books first and take it from there?' The idea was such a success that even before the month of July, all the books were sold out and we got reprint orders three to four times. My father was impressed that Ramesh had come up with a very good business idea. Later, they started printing books right up to Class 10 and the business grew. My own impression was that my brother always had it in him to keep expanding the business. But my father didn't listen to him most of the time."

"By the time Bhaisaab finished his studies, he was already helping my father with the business. Their views didn't match at all and my father would keep Bhaisaab under his thumb, *dabaake rakhte thay*. It was only when my father angrily left the business to my brother and said, do what you want to do with it, that Bhaisaab came into his own and showed his mettle. By then my brother was already married and had children of his own."

When brother Ramesh Chandra wed Sharda Garg in great style on 8 May 1965 and brought her home, they called the new entrant Bhabhiji (the 'ji' added to distinguish her from Bhabhi which was how they addressed their mother). The flamboyant Dwarka Prasad had invited world-renowned *shehnai* (Indian clarinet) player Ustad Bismillah Khan to perform at the wedding of his only son.

Traditionally, women wouldn't go with the *baraat* (the groom's party), so Meena got her first glimpse of Bhabhiji only when she came home as a newlywed. 21-year-old Ramesh Chandra too hadn't seen his own bride until they were married. His first son, Sudhir (Guddu) was born two years later in 1967.

The family still had Keshav Bhavan, their house in Gosaipura in Jhansi, eponymously named after Dwarka Prasad's father. That was the house where Sharda Devi entered the Agarwal *parivaar* (family) as a young bride. Meena was about 17-18 years old when her sister-in-law arrived. Keshav Bhavan was also where Meena was later married to Dr Suresh Garg.

Fortunately for Ramesh Chandra, his wife and his sister hit it off from the outset. "In our family, if the daughter made a mistake, it was overlooked. But if the daughter-in-law did something wrong, there would be mayhem," explained Meena. "I didn't like my sister-in-law getting scolded when something went wrong. Once, the rice she made was slightly undercooked and my father roared, 'Who has made this rice?' I piped up and took the responsibility for it. My father's only response to that was, 'Okay, be careful henceforth.' Bhabhiji was very happy that I'd taken the rap."

Once the new Bhabhi was welcomed into the family, Meena went back to her studies. But Dwarka Prasad thought it an utter waste of time and would stop his children from sitting for exams. Girls didn't need to study, they were better off learning to cook and run a house. In his view, they were going to get married and go away anyway.

Dwarka Prasad's views on his son's education too were those of a traditional *bania.* Sons, according to him, would eventually go into business and studies wouldn't help them become businessmen.

Childhood had its share of amusing moments too. Like the time Ramesh Chandra, like a responsible older brother, got Meena admitted to Sultaniya School in Bhopal. But in his naivete, he put his own date of birth on her form instead of hers.

It led to much hilarity. The Principal wondered why Meena was in a lower class when she was so much older. Meena had no idea; she also had no clue when her birthday was. The school sent a notice to Dwarka Prasad who thundered, "What did you go and write in her school?"

Ramesh had to go back to Meena's school, apologise and correct the mistake he had inadvertently made.

He had a quirk too in his childhood. If he wasn't enjoying a particular game with friends, he would insist on going back home and drag his sisters along, much against their wishes. They would then play *gilli-danda* and *kanche* (simple, traditional Indian games) with him at home. "He always wanted to win and because we were much younger than him, he would invariably do so and be jubilant over his victory. Of course, I would fight with him over it," Meena laughed.

"Around 1980, Bhaisaab started doing well professionally. He would say that to grow big, you have to start small. However small the start, he was always confident that he would one day become a very successful man."

Meena was the one who could best comment on what spurred Ramesh Chandra to reach for the skies.

"He inherited a very good quality from my father. He wouldn't get defeated, *woh haarte nahin thay*. My father was also like that. Whatever the setback, he would stand tall and go at it again. Earlier, because I was frightened of my father, I stayed neutral but after a really huge fight they had in 1982, all of us had to take sides. My husband and I were clear that we would always be with my brother. The family split into two groups, my father went away to Gwalior. We stood with my brother and that's how it was till the very end."

For all the amity and family unity, friction was always around the corner.

For a mild-mannered man, Ramesh Chandra knew that the differences between his father and him went far beyond their contrasting personalities. He had understood this in the '70s itself when he was still cowering in the shadow of the towering elder. One of the many responsibilities he shouldered was to go forth and seek ad support from major cities where the big commercial players operated.

Those were times when, existing solely on the benevolence of ads from the state government, and a few low-cost local ones, newspapers in an underdeveloped state like Madhya Pradesh did not attract the attention of the corporate world.

Like its other publications in the market, DB too was printed on pulp paper made available under a government quota. If truth be told, the lowly produced black-and-white DB was shabby in appearance and sold in such feeble numbers that it didn't figure anywhere in the ABC (Audit Bureau of Circulation) charts.

So, when Ramesh Chandra would set off to the big cities on a small and controlled budget allotted by his father, he would brace himself for the derision that he would invariably face from ad agencies and corporate advertisers. Their message to him rarely varied. It was: spruce up the look of your newspaper and beef up its circulation figures before you come to us again.

That was the prevailing equation between DB and the advertisers when he went to Bombay in 1978 armed with a letter of recommendation from former Chief Minister Prakash Chandra Sethi to leading industrialists Dhirubhai Ambani and Nusli Wadia. That introduction was the turning point in Ramesh Chandra's life.

He returned with cheques that totalled Rs 20,000 which was big money in those days. But of bigger worth was the invaluable piece of advice that Dhirubhai handed to the young newspaperman seated before him. 'A good business is one that can run independently. It should not just cover its cost but also improve the lives of its owners and its employees,' said Dhirubhai to him.

The monthly operational cost of the Bhopal edition of DB

was Rs 35,000. So when Ramesh Chandra returned home with such a hefty cheque, his father was jubilant. Ramesh was not.

"Papa felt humiliated," recalled Pawan who had heard the story from his father. "He asked himself, 'Am I going to live off charity and donations to run my newspaper?'

"The Dhirubhai Ambani episode had bruised his self-respect. It hurt him deeply that he was given the money because somebody had told Ambani to do so and not because he deserved it or had earned it. He vowed never to put himself in such a situation again."

His brushes with the corporate world and their advertising agencies had seared Ramesh Chandra's self-respect and the words of Dhirubhai Ambani rang clearly in his mind. He knew that his targets and those of his father would never match: to continue in the newspaper business, he had to make DB self-reliant, sustain itself and stand on its own two feet.

For Dwarka Prasad, DB was not his main source of income. Being a newspaperman gave him societal dignity in the corridors of power. So he had editions coming out of Bhopal, Jhansi, Gwalior and Ujjain which put him several rungs higher than other businessmen on the social ladder. However, none of his papers made enough money to cover even the cost of production.

For Ramesh Chandra, the corporate brushes steered him towards the goals that he had set for his beloved newspaper. The first, as the metro meetings had harshly told him, was to make DB undergo cosmetic surgery and get a face-lift. Therefore, his earliest move was to discard museum pieces like the Varityper (word processor of the pre-digital era) that was used for the Bhopal edition and the Cylinder printer which spewed the Ujjain edition. He bought the DB group's first offset machine to Bhopal and introduced huge new-age cameras for photo processing, replacing block technology. In 1980, the text began to be composed on computers which was another big leap towards modernising the newspaper.

Soon, DB got a makeover that made it stand out stylishly from other regional language papers in the market. Until then, they were all leap years behind English newspapers in technology and marketing. Satisfied that his paper was looking sophisticated, Ramesh Chandra could tick off the first box of two that the big players of the advertising world had told him to take care of before getting in touch with them again.

His next professional compulsion was to increase the circulation figures of his Hindi language paper. Having not just multiple editions of DB but also an impressive presence in a commercial city was imperative to his game plan.

It was a pretty pathetic scenario. Treated like proverbial stepchildren, regional newspapers nursed an inferiority complex and stayed self-effacingly in their own little shells. English newspapers comprised the creamy layer that everybody looked up to, and nobody would even dream of galloping in the same race as them.

There was also a strange compromise that the Indian language newspapers had reached amongst themselves. Like small-time dons who operated in their own territories, each newspaper had its own little fiefdom, beyond which it wouldn't put out even a toe. By not venturing out of their demarcated areas, they not just felt protected and safe but also stayed impractically insulated from the real world.

That was when the second clash took place in the family business arena, as Ramesh Chandra looked to cast his net outside Bhopal.

Indore was the commercial capital of Madhya Pradesh and in such an important city, DB was a non-player. There were only two newspapers that really counted in undivided Madhya Pradesh (before it bifurcated into Chattisgarh and MP in 2000)—*Navbharat* and *Nai Duniya.* While the former boasted multi-editions, the latter, which was Indore-based, was the undisputed emperor of the region.

Nai Duniya, established by Babu Labhchand Chhajlani, Narendra Tiwari and Vasantilal Sethia, had become as addictive as their morning cup of tea for many of its readers. It had acquired cult status as an institution in journalism and was eagerly awaited even if it reached other districts a day later.

Dwarka Prasad had a small bureau office in Khajuri Bazaar, on MG Road in Indore, to collect advertisements for DB's Bhopal, Ujjain and Gwalior editions. Manned by two staffers, there was no rate card for ads, which would be arbitrarily decided by the advertiser and the ad agencies. It was a classic case of take-it-or-leave-it and DB gratefully accepted whatever it was offered. Sometimes, the two staffers would take away a few ads from *Nai Duniya* and pass them on to DB. It was a haphazard way of functioning.

Ramesh Chandra liked order and systems. So he put into action a step-by-step plan to pull DB out of anonymity and gave it numero uno status. His first firm resolve was to go to Indore and take on the reigning newspaper king. He asked his Chartered Accountant friend Ravi Sethi to put together a project, apply for a loan of Rs 25 lakh and make sure the loan got sanctioned. Whatever the consequences, he was ready for it.

This was the tableau when Ramesh Chandra decided to beard *Nai Duniya* in its own den. Multi-city editions of DB with a strong presence in a commercial city was the only route to achieving his goal of making his paper a self-reliant, financially viable business venture.

The suggestion was shot down by his father.

But with obstinacy etched deep in both their systems, each stayed seething in his own corner until Dwarka Prasad finally blinked—with conditions attached. Ramesh Chandra needed margin money until the loan came through. His father gave him the money with the warning that he was not going to underwrite this suicidal mission. He told his 39-year-old son, 'Go, do it at your own peril. The risk will be yours and yours alone.'

Dwarka Prasad's apprehensions were not unfounded. In 1983, *Nai Duniya* had a circulation of 1.4 lakh in Indore alone while all the other newspapers put together stood at an anemic 50,000. *Nai Duniya* was so gigantic and powerful that all the midgets around it would bow low and seek its permission before finalising their own cover price or ad rate. Agents and hawkers were also too awestruck and would be reluctant to pick up any other newspaper for fear of upsetting the *Nai Duniya* applecart. The same spirit of spinelessness prevailed in advertising agencies that wouldn't dare give equal terms to any other publication.

But Ramesh Chandra had come armed with determination and plans for an offensive. With the loan of Rs 25 lakh that he'd got from the Madhya Pradesh Finance Corporation, he reached Indore with his cousin Manmohan Agarwal by his side. Ramesh Chandra wasn't naïve, he had his ear to the ground and he had already caught the low rumblings of many high-profile residents and families who were disgruntled with *Nai Duniya's* biased political slant. The rumblings translated into discreet support for anyone who could stand up to and challenge the ruling royalty. Ramesh Chandra picked up the gauntlet and the families who knew about him welcomed him with behind-the-scenes assistance.

"Launching the Indore edition was the toughest battle the company had faced thus far. Compared to *Nai Duniya*, we were nowhere. It was like a 1:100 equation between us," tracked Sudhir. "I was 15 years old then, but my grandfather told my father to make me the manager of the Bhopal office. When my father pointed out that I was too young to sign cheques, Dadaji called up Guptaji the bank manager and told him, 'Do whatever you can, but cheques will be signed only by Sudhir.' So I started signing cheques and became the manager of the Bhopal end of the business. My grandfather had sheer guts."

Ramesh Chandra was not far behind in courage and he knew

where to start digging: he needed land in the press complex. He got a piece for Rs1,00,000 and built Bhaskar Bhavan, procured water and electricity connections, appointed staff and established the printing plant. Nothing happened overnight or with ease as there were hurdles to overcome at every turn. He had taken on an established name, one with a very long reach. To get his first copy out was going to take a long time and the journey wasn't on even terrain, it was rocky and slippery. Permissions were required at every step. But by the time he got around one officer for a green signal and moved to the next, he would learn that what had been sanctioned earlier had been nullified. Shunting frenetically between Indore and Bhopal, a lesser player would've wilted but the Vaish businessman in him wouldn't back off. Every challenge acted as a spur. And every bit of it was enriching as he learnt at every step of the way.

There was a sense of accomplishment on 5 March 1983.

Chief Minister Arjun Singh and Union Minister HKL Bhagat were welcomed by an animated line-up of hosts that included patriarch Dwarka Prasad and Ramesh Chandra with his sons. Sudhir was a mere boy of 16, Girish was still to turn 13 and Pawan was only 10 years old.

The hospitality was typical of the hearty Agarwals. 2,000 guests were served sweets that were sourced all the way from Banaras, Calcutta and Agra, as they watched the launch of DB's Indore edition.

However, while the launch packed a punch, the paper didn't. It was not the most impressive of newspapers but Ramesh Chandra had done something right. Sharad Jain of Dulichand and Sons whose grandfather (after whom the firm was named) had once hawked newspapers in Indore in 1918 and had set up an agency for newspapers and magazines in 1924, pointed towards a very pertinent fact, one that put DB ahead of other contenders. "Having been associated with this business for over 37 years, we know the promoters and owners of all the newspapers and magazines," he said. "But, as my father the Late Trilokchand Jain used to say, Ramesh Chandra Agarwal was the only newspaper owner who not only understood the role of agents and hawkers in the publishing business but also taught many others how important this menial-looking link in the chain was. Every member of the Agarwal family has met us and our associates with humility. They would ask us our opinion about the newspaper and also take from us the feedback of readers. Even before the first print of the Indore edition could reach the market, Rameshji was present at our shop."

He added that even after DB became the newspaper with the largest circulation, he had the same freedom from the Agarwal family to inform them, whatever be the time, even wake them up if the newspaper was delayed in the market. "Whenever we have called Rameshji or Sudhirji on their cell phones, even if it was 3 am we have found the local management of DB reaching the spot in no time to take matters in hand," he disclosed.

Though the newspaper itself was not earth-shatteringly exciting in content, readers were impressed that the first edition came with a booklet on the history of Indore. But there was little else to suggest that DB's editorial content was creating a *nai duniya* (new world) of its own. Dwarka Prasad sneeringly predicted that his son would pack his bags from Indore and return to Bhopal within six months.

Ramesh Chandra himself did an honest appraisal and wasn't quite impressed with what he'd created. But to quit as his father had forecast was not even a thought, he found a workable solution instead. He picked Dr Yatindra Bhatnagar from the *Hindustan Times* and handed him the editorial responsibility of the Indore edition. This move was without parallel—no other newspaper in Madhya Pradesh had so far hired a full-time professional editor.

This was another of Ramesh Chandra's skills—to look for talent outside his realm and bring them into the DB fold. Dr Bhatnagar, proficient in Hindi, English, French and Chinese, was a seasoned editor. The much-respected Dr Om Nagpal was also a DB editor until he was appointed member of UGC (University Grants Commission, a government body).

Ramesh Chandra had another natural asset that he put to good use: he trusted people and knew how to delegate responsibility. While he shuttled between Bhopal and Indore, cousin Manmohan Agarwal managed the daily operations.

"When he launched the Indore edition in 1983, he took me with him," Manmohan rewound. "I didn't know the ABC, the basics of a newspaper, nothing about editorial content or advertisements. He first put me in charge of production.

"Three months later, he pointed me towards the editorial department and then made me look at the editorial content and news. Later, he shifted me to the management side. In this way, within six months, I was looking after the entire newspaper. Rameshji also sent me into town to meet people and introduced me around. My meeting with people gave new energy to DB. It grew rapidly within two years."

He gave an example of how his more experienced cousin looked at the newspaper.

"On one or two occasions, I had printed some sensational news on the front page. After such story, some so-called *shubh chintaks* (well-wishers) in Indore complained to him early in the morning and he fired me over the phone from Bhopal."

The story that had stirred a hornet's nest was about a popular vegetable oil that mixed mutton tallow in it during the refining process. Naming the company, Manmohan had a headline blazing across the front page which told its readers that the pure vegetarian Jain community's religious sentiments had been hurt by this oil company.

Fortunately, Ramesh Chandra was scheduled to make a pitstop at Ujjain and what he heard there saved the day for Manmohan.

"In Ujjain, Bhaisaab heard people praising the story DB had published. It was a credible story that we had carried and he was pleased that people were complimenting him for it. So by the time he reached Indore, he was saying, 'You must publish such stories. Why should we fear anybody if the news is true?'" He grinned as he recollected the good old times. For Ramesh Chandra, what mattered was that his readers had approved of it wholeheartedly. The reader was the leader.

Having understood that influential readers were veering away from *Nai Duniya* because of the imbalance in its political reporting, Ramesh Chandra spent more time networking and getting to know what people expected from a newspaper. What he was sure of was that his newspaper wouldn't be a forum for politicians alone but would also throw light on social issues. His guideline to the editorial staff was, "Prioritise news and photos in accordance with their news value and in the interests of the newspaper. Reach the spot, assess the truth in a story and don't worry about the consequences."

Those dissatisfied with *Nai Duniya* became the unwitting brand ambassadors of DB as their words of praise pushed it into the limelight.

But a complication in existing equations threatened to halt the prevailing bliss.

"When DB started growing, the tussle between our families escalated," recalled Manmohan, who had to make a choice between staying by his cousin's side or throwing his all with his father and brothers. He chose the latter.

But what would have been a major upset for most people was a minor hiccup for Ramesh Chandra who dealt with it with characteristic composure. He made only one move—he replaced

Manmohan with his 19-year-old son Sudhir and business continued uninterrupted. What he did was a throwback to what his father had done—of getting his son into the business while he was still a teenager.

In 1986, three years after launching his daily in Indore, he introduced Sudhir to the basics and the finer aspects of bringing out a newspaper and two years later, handed independent charge of the new edition to him. In his lifetime, Ramesh Chandra credited his wife with this move. Sharda Devi who had gauged Sudhir's worth had told her husband, 'Sudhir is the one who'll fulfill all your ambitions, he's ready for the job.' It was a career-decision that gave Ramesh Chandra immense satisfaction.

By pulling off the challenge he'd thrown at an established paper, Ramesh Chandra Agarwal planted the DB flag firmly in the newspaper industry of Madhya Pradesh, driven by the strongest trait that makes men scale seemingly unconquerable peaks: an uncommon but inescapable sense of adventure and fearlessness. Going into Indore had been a gamble, he had put property and credibility at stake.

But he was lucky too. Sudhir had such a nose for news that his skills at sizing up the relevance of a story, playing it up by placing it on the appropriate page and laying it out with flair became legendary in the editorial world. Sudhir hired creative graphic designer Nishit Sharan at a time when even sophisticated English newspapers did not lay emphasis on the layout of their editorial content.

One such historical front page that remained unparalleled was the way the news of Rajiv Gandhi's assassination was presented in DB.

Rajiv Gandhi was assassinated in Sriperumbudur near Chennai on 25 May 1991 when the editorial team at DB was headless at the time with the post of Resident Editor lying vacant. So the senior editorial team rose to the task, collected a bunch of interesting photographs and collated all the relevant information on Rajiv Gandhi's political journey, memorable vignettes from his life and his startling assassination during an election campaign. But they hit a mental block over how to present this important story in a way that it would make readers sit up and take notice, and appreciate it.

The team finally came up with a bold, but radically different idea. While any conventional man at the top would have rejected such a move outright, Sudhir gave it a thumbs up. And the next day, DB flashed the assassination of Rajiv Gandhi right at the top of the front page, shifting its own logo and masthead to the middle of the page. It was such an eye-catching and innovating idea that readers burst into applause.

But Sudhir had learnt from his father's captaincy. He knew that as far back as 1983, when DB was still taking tentative steps in a new world and every source of revenue was welcome, Ramesh Chandra had put news over commercials on the day the Indian cricket team had proudly lifted the World Cup. The sports team at DB had collected a treasurable cache of captivating photographs and reports. But that day, just when the editorial team had a great story to play up, there were more advertisements pencilled in than was normal for the sports page. Fortunately, Ramesh Chandra Agarwal was present in Indore. When the sports desk shared with him their concerns that their story would be drowned by the ads on the page, his first reaction was that of any conventional publisher. 'Removing advertisements is akin to picking one's own pocket,' he growled, as he got up and began walking towards the pasting desk with the team following closely behind. When he saw the content that his team had put together on the World Cup, he wordlessly removed the advertisements himself. To him, what the readers wanted was paramount.

He thus fully nourished DB's identity as a readers' paper,

and not one that existed solely to fill its own coffers. Reciprocally, the growing community of readers boosted the circulation and made it quite trendy to be a DB subscriber.

Illustrious IAS officer and retired Chief of TRAI (Telecom Regulation Authority of India) Pradip Baijal from the MP cadre met the man from Bhopal who'd burst upon the newspaper scene in Indore and a warm acquaintance grew between them.

A keen watcher of the newspaper business, Baijal said, "In 1966, I was posted in Khandwa which is very close to Indore. The only newspaper that mattered in MP at that time was *Nai Duniya*. It was like a gazetteer. No paper could come close to it. If *Nai Duniya* decided to take a stand, that became the government policy. It was so powerful."

It's a belief that if you desire something passionately enough, the universe will conspire to create circumstances that work in your favour. *Nai Duniya* was beset with internal problems around the time Ramesh Chandra put a toe into Indore.

"There were other newspapers in Madhya Pradesh. *Bhaskar, Jagran, Hithvad, MP Chronicle*. But when *Nai Duniya* went down, it was *Dainik Bhaskar* that picked up and did so at great speed," observed Baijal.

It was, of course, not only about the universe granting favours but also about the man at the helm who drove DB to dizzying heights, bringing in changes that would transform the way advertisers and the world of readers would look at a regional newspaper.

"I was always interested in studying newspapers," Baijal divulged. "So I went to Mr Agarwal and asked him how they'd risen so fast. He explained that they had a policy to never mix scandal with news, to give a balanced viewpoint and to try and be correct all the time."

'Don't mix views with news', was one of Ramesh Chandra's maxims which worked. Group Editor Kalpesh Yagnik who had begun his career as city chief, remembered how unrelentingly Ramesh Chandra would question the objectivity of a story. "On a sensitive dispute on Dewas Mata (a deity), he directed many strong questions at me. Who brought this news? Can a reporter be trusted so much? Can *Bhaskar* publish such a report?

"But when he found that there was truth in the news, he was equally aggressive in saying, 'Go ahead and publish it. Whether the matter pertains to faith, religion or anything else, the readers must get what's true,'" Kalpesh said, revealing what all had gone into putting DB on a fearless, winning path.

Former Chief Election Commissioner, OP Rawat, a seasoned bureaucrat had seen Ramesh Chandra morph from a Jhansi lad into a newspaper baron.

"I knew him from his and my birth place, Jhansi," said Rawat. "The only difference was that he was born nine years before me.

"When Rameshji left for Bhopal, I must have been around 14 and he about 22 or 23. He would come to attend functions like Diwali in Jhansi and we would often meet. Jhansi is a small place with barely a handful of youngsters who were doing well. Individuals like him were few and far between, so you could easily identify them and you could tell that they would be the ones who would one day make a difference.

"On one of the Diwalis when he was visiting Jhansi, post the Bhopal launch, Rameshji was very critical of firecrackers," remembered Rawat. "This practice should be stopped, he would say. Why are we polluting the air? That kind of social concern was in him from an early age itself."

It was in Indore that they connected again when OP Rawat was posted there as Collector.

"It was Mr Agarwal who first informed me that I had been appointed Collector of Indore," he smiled. "He had already started his Indore edition, so he had found out that there was this lad from Jhansi who was coming into the city as Collector."

Evidently, Ramesh Chandra's famous networking was already in place in Indore although, "He was facing stiff competition there, dominated by another paper which was doing very well. Creating a space for yourself in such an atmosphere was tough but he managed so well that the other paper (*Nai Duniya*) had to be eventually sold to *Dainik Jagran.*"

Rawat also discovered that Ramesh Chandra watched out for 'the other lad from Jhansi' in very subtle ways. "As I was the Collector, he knew that his close association with me could create problems for me with the other media house. So, even though I wanted to meet him more frequently, he would excuse himself saying he was busy. He would have some excuse or the other not to meet me. It was only later that I understood that he did this only to protect my interests. His view was that as Collector I needed the support of the other strong media houses too and his friendship with me should not come in the way.

"I was there for more than two years and during that period, I really felt that he was like a guardian figure for me. Because we were both from the same place and he was older than me, he felt he had to protect me. Yes, there were times when DB was critical of me but I realised that what he had published was right."

All of this pointed to a unique combination of strengths—of a man who could be a newspaper professional with not just sharp business instincts but also the ability to balance friendships with an honest editorial policy.

But Ramesh Chandra as the head had two arms that reinforced the DB structure. One was Sudhir. Like his father, Sudhir had the gift of a *bania* brain that kept track of costs without compromising on quality. Earlier, news and photographs would be put into envelopes and sent through carriers who'd go by bus to physically deliver them to DB's other offices. Sudhir decided to open bureau offices in the smaller cities and towns and set up modems to enhance accuracy and speed. Editorial content could be now shared by the main editions in a time-saving and cost-effective manner. This change in the dissemination of information made DB the first with the news of the day and with this, the readership swelled.

The other arm was the sustained marketing which tantalised advertisers, a domain where his second son, Girish, showed early signs of virtuosity. Instead of outsourcing the processs of collecting ads, DB went independent and was the first vernacular newspaper to establish a vast marketing network in the metros and in the rural areas. The latter saw a spurt in employment opportunities for the rural youth.

Under Girish's baton, 'Tiger' was one of DB's visually dramatic campaigns. All it showed was a pouncing tiger with the line, 'You are seeing our only competitor in Madhya Pradesh'.

Madhya Pradesh would see DB in every corner as Jabalpur, Raipur and Bilaspur editions were also launched over the next few years.

Celebrations with readers and advertisers discreetly boosted the brand with *Bhaskar Utsav*. The presence of crowd-drawing celebrities like Shah Rukh Khan, Aishwarya Rai, Late TN Seshan and Late KPS Gill at the *Utsav* drummed up enthusiasm in youngsters and popularised *Bhaskar* across the board.

In 1992, it was a victorious moment for Ramesh Chandra Agarwal when he received the latest market survey—DB was the newspaper with the highest readership in Indore. DB had knocked down *Nai Duniya* from its comfortable perch and become the addictive daily cuppa of the largest city in Madhya Pradesh.

The 9 years between 1983 and 1992 were years of tumult and triumph, of landmark successes at the workplace and painful surgical separations at home. 9 eventful years nonetheless, whichever way you looked at it.

Chapter 2

FEUDS & THE FIRST STEP

'There comes a time when you have to choose between turning the page and closing the book'

—Anon

1984 was an Orwellian year.

In October, 1984: Indira Gandhi was assassinated, leading to riots and a horrific anti-Sikh genocide.

In December, 1984: the Bhopal Gas Tragedy struck the hapless city and killed scores of people mercilessly, while the government escorted the corporate culprits of the disaster to safety, out of the country.

The twin tragedies waltzed grotesquely together to enter the lives of one family and wreak havoc.

'If it bleeds, it leads' is a cruel, centuries-old newspaper adage that unfortunately holds true any place, any time.

The Bhopal Gas Tragedy of 1984 was an accident that had been forewarned but was swept aside by a Union Carbide subsidiary pesticide plant in the city of Bhopal. On the fateful night of 2 December 1984, the plant spewed approximately 40 tonnes of methyl isocyanate (MIC) gas into the air, exposing more than 5,00,000 people to the deadly poison.

This was when *Dainik Bhaskar* still operated from Ibrahimpura in the old city, a locality which was one of the worst hit by the toxic gas. Ramesh Chandra Agarwal was at work when he recognised the opportunity at his doorstep and decided to grab it by its neck. He and a few courageous colleagues of his stepped out into the hellish dance of death unfolding around the city, to try and find stories that authenticated and asserted the sheer magnitude of the disaster. It bore fruit, instantly.

When the next day dawned, DB was the sole newspaper which had first-hand reports supported by visually telling photographs of the chilling disaster. RC Sahu from DB became the only photographer in the world to have clicked and collected a library of rare photos of dazed, blinded victims–hundreds of men, women and children in the throes of death–running *en masse,* gasping for a breath of fresh air, desperate to somehow save their lives. Unmindful of the danger to their own selves, Sahu and reporter Rajesh Chanchal had ventured out into the vile air and the hapless crowds, so that they could record those apocalyptic moments for posterity.

Ramesh Chandra was not satiated, he knew there was more to tell and was restless. That DB had already put out more than what other newspapers had was not a consolation he was willing to accept. There were rumours that the Union Carbide plant had not contained the leak, there was danger of another. Ramesh Chandra wanted more action from DB.

On 3 December 1984, he called an emergency meeting of his editorial team to motivate them to go back into the field.

Though Aleem Bazmi, an employee of many years who was present at the meeting couldn't recall the exact words after the lapse of several decades, he did remember the gist of what was said at the meeting. "Bhaisaab (Ramesh Chandra) said, 'Death spares no one and it never discriminates. What is unfortunate is that laxity of administration and human error are behind this accident. It could have been avoided. Our profession is similar to that of the armed forces. A true soldier does not lay down arms without fighting.' Rameshji asked those present at the meeting not to run away from the scene, to take stock of the situation and to do their duty. He assured the staffers that DB would take care of them and their families."

With such an emphatic call to arms, the DB family turned into a platoon of soldiers with even peons and machine operators fanning out to collect news. Every bit of information was given attention but by now, the citizens of Bhopal themselves began to approach DB, the one paper that was listening to them, giving them a voice and doing them justice. Moving, tragic stories of pain and suffering came pouring out from victims and their families, making it an emotionally stirring experience for the DB staff.

The paper set a record by publishing over 100 photos in its 12-page edition. The visuals were so compelling that it looked like 'television in print'. The editorial team began collecting evidence of administrative lapses and it was only DB that enterprisingly found out and published the horrifying news that the poisonous gas was still being produced at the plant. It forewarned the people and the authorities that the city could once again turn into a gas chamber at any moment.

Apart from bringing to the fore the irregularities in the plant, the indifference of the authorities and the collusion of influential people with political leaders, DB also informed its readers what the gas was all about; how poisonous and dangerous it was, how it would adversely impact the future and what could be done to safeguard oneself and the city from its debilitating after-effects.

There was a virtual storm when DB covered with much detail the arrival of Warren H Anderson, the Chairman of Union Carbide, his all-too brief judicial custody and his questionable exit from the country under the government's protection. DB raised questions in the minds of the people and the open scrutiny made the political dispensation squirm uncomfortably.

However, Ramesh Chandra Agarwal did not remain just another newspaperman doing his job and benefiting from it. His conscience gave him another duty—to ensure that camps were set up at various places to offer assistance to the affected people. To this day, many remember that DB's camps were organised even before the government stepped in to do its duty.

DB's coverage of the tragedy with all its ramifications was so extensive and informative that BBC and other international media began to look to this paper for authentic news and updates on the Bhopal gas leak disaster. DB's reports were also produced in courts where the case against Union Carbide was heard. The international, local and legal demand for photographic evidence was so high that Bhaskar's library was left with no photographs for their own reference. This was the pre-digital era where hard copies were distributed and rarely returned after use. Those exclusive images not only provided heartrending visuals to news stories of the tragedy in various newspapers and magazines, an exhibition of the photographs was also held in America.

The consistent and relentless reporting led to a tremor in the administration which reached Delhi where Rajiv Gandhi was the Prime Minister. He had taken over after his mother's assassination and was only a few months into his new job when the Bhopal Gas Tragedy happened. He was still a political novice while Arjun Singh, the Chief Minister of Madhya Pradesh, was wily, powerful and important both in the state and at the national level. The PM and the Congress Party leaned on the support and advice of stalwarts like him. At that time, DB was an insignificant player. *Nav Bharat* had multi-city editions, while the much-respected *Nai Duniya* carried the most weight. Ramesh Chandra had only just made his foray into Indore and was still a fledgling at the game.

In such a scenario, he began to receive messages that went from softly veiled to openly loud; clear warnings to tone down the strong editorial content. These threats from the government in power were sometimes dressed up as well-meant advice but the message remained the same: go easy with the reporting. DB, however, continued undeterred. Ramesh Chandra was a man on fire. It wasn't long before the powerful Arjun Singh called him for a meeting. It was an eye-to-eye David and Goliath confrontation.

When Ramesh Chandra reached the CM's house, Arjun Singh made his point in a diplomatic way. He told the DB Chairman that whatever had happened was tragic and that he was more concerned and saddened than anybody else. 'But we have to answer the people, assist them and help them win back their self-worth. Since the situation requires great compassion, I suggest that we work together. The government is on the verge of initiating relief measures on a large scale. You are requested to pitch in and help too.'

Ramesh Chandra knew where this conversation was going, so he minced no words in his counter to the CM. 'Sir,' he said, 'whatever happened has indeed been unfortunate. But even more worrisome is the fact that this accident could have been averted. Complacence and laxity have been witnessed at all levels and unfortunately, it is evident even today. We can support the relief measures to be initiated by the government but we cannot make a commitment about our reporting on the matter. The tradition of DB is to ensure that news reaches the reader unfiltered.'

Arjun Singh was seasoned at political deals and manoeuvres. Wearing an inscrutable expression, he took out his handkerchief and began cleaning his spectacles. There was a short spell of tense silence after which Singh advised him to have 'a practical approach'.

After sticking to his guns however mighty the man he faced, Ramesh Chandra returned to his office feeling the pressure and the stress of such a strained meeting. It had been a clear 'do as we tell you or else' warning from the CM of the state.

The editorial team awaited his return and Ramesh Chandra called a meeting immediately. He addressed his team and told his staff, 'If we do not abide by the advice (read threats) of the Chief Minister, then we have to be prepared for a backlash. There may be inconveniences like disconnection of water and power. There could be disruptions in the publication and distribution of our newspaper. The government may stop its advertisements to DB. Everything that happened to Ramnath Goenka and *The Indian Express* during the Emergency could happen to us.' He ran the implications of his decision through his mind and added thoughtfully, 'I can run this newspaper without advertisements for a year.'

They knew the fallout would be enormous but the editorial staff was unanimous in its support for the enthused young owner. Ramesh Chandra was only 40 and was still to become a name to reckon with. But his courage was reflected in his staff as they decided in one voice, 'We'll fight this people's battle without fear. We're ready to face whatever comes our way, however unpleasant or terrifying it may be.'

Seeing the resoluteness of his team, Ramesh Chandra declared, 'Let the news be published as it is. Leave no stone unturned to ensure that truth prevails in our news reports. From today, DB will be accountable only to its readers, we will give them what they want.'

Madhya Pradesh saw two kinds of newspapers thereafter. One toed the line, edited out the primary cause of the accident and its aftermath and spotlighted only the relief measures initiated by the government, thereby becoming the voice of the administration. DB chose to be the voice of the people. Every move to thwart and intimidate him, toughened Ramesh Chandra's resolve.

And from the ashes of the tragedy rose 'The people's newspaper'. In a very short spell, DB became the No. 1 newspaper of Bhopal, its circulation outstripping that of all its rival publications. It laid the foundation for Ramesh Chandra's mantra for eternity: give the reader what he wants.

The tragedy had claimed thousands of innocent lives and tens of thousands had been painfully mutilated and damaged forever. DB pulled up those responsible for it and provided a platform for people to vent their grievances. It was DB's consistency, its courage to challenge and its credibility that gave a dramatic push to its sales.

It was also a double-edged moment because while the circulation soared, the backlash from the government was severe. Thus, there was a balance. Ramesh Chandra paid a heavy price for his fearless editorial stand but earned the loyalty of a large and growing readership.

Sudhir put the cost of the spirited reporting at approximately Rs 5 lakh at that time, calculated on the basis of the ads that were blocked and not given to DB. It was a huge loss of revenue in the 80s but what Ramesh Chandra gained was incalculable. Playing politics or partisan reporting went out of the window forever as the reader and his wants became the fundamentals of DB's editorial policy. 'The reader is the leader' became the company chant.

It would be pertinent to point out that in this quest to remain apolitical, Ramesh Chandra also turned down the offer of a seat in the Rajya Sabha a few years down the line and simultaneously laid the thumb rule that no member of the DB family would ever be associated with any political party. A political alignment would not only create a doubt in the minds of readers but editorial objectivity would also get tossed out in the bargain.

The success of the DB group and the management acumen of its Chairman would one day become a case study at some of the world's top business schools including Harvard Business Review and IIM, Ahmedabad and Bengaluru.

But in 1985, Ramesh Chandra had a shakier bridge to cross, one that would lead to resentment, estrangement and realignment of personal affiliations.

The turn in their fortunes found Ramesh Chandra's family moving out of Ibrahimpura and taking up residence in a sprawling bungalow in the upmarket Arera Colony. That was in June, 1985. By October in the same year, DB also built the most prestigious and top-end office in all of Bhopal. Two moves that did not go well with his uncles.

What followed was, in a nutshell:

In 1985, trouble brewed between Ramesh Chandra and his uncle, leading to a settlement in 1986. But it once again reared its head in 1987.

In 1987-88, Arjun Singh, still bristling over the 1984 coverage, sided with his uncle Vishambhar Dayal and father Dwarka Prasad Agarwal, to make life unspeakably harrowing for Ramesh Chandra. Singh was the CM from 1980-85. He was sent to Punjab as Governor in 1985 but returned to MP where he once again ruled as CM from 1988-89.

From 1987-92, the family disputes were heard in court.

'People will rate you, hate you, shake you and break you but how strong you stand is what makes you', is a popular saying.

How strong he stood was what made Ramesh Chandra Agarwal the man he was.

Dipping into his sharp memory, Sudhir detailed the messy and very costly family drama with its roller-coaster emotions, uncles and cousins in the fray over property, business and legitimacy.

"Problems really surfaced only after 1985 when we built the DB office," Sudhir said, as he traced the source of familial tension. "Till 1983, my father and all of us were extremely docile. My uncle and his family had moved into a big house of their own but my father was the least ambitious man around. He bought personal peace by never bothering to buy a car, new clothes or even a stereo system for the house. He had no hobbies except watching movies and his life revolved around his business. So there were no disputes."

He continued, "We were still living in the rooftop rooms of that old building in Ibrahimpura and operating from the old office. When I entered the business as the Manager for Bhopal, I began to tell Papa that when people come to visit us, we should have at least a good drawing room. So let's get ourselves a proper house of our own. In 1984, there were riots in Bhopal after Mrs Gandhi died. During the gas tragedy, Bhopal was like a tinderbox and Ibrahimpura was not the ideal area to be in at that time. That was the year I told my father that we really needed to move out. In June 1985, we moved into a rented but nice big bungalow in Arera Colony. In October, we moved to our sprawling DB office in MP Nagar.

"Until then we didn't have any disputes with my father's uncles. They did their business and we carried on with ours. But once our new office sprang up, everybody suddenly realised that DB had become a prosperous business. A dispute started within the family. We settled it with them by dividing territories, like Jabalpur and Nagpur, where they started bringing out the paper. But in 1987, there was trouble again. There was a massive and very ugly fight with my grandfather and his brother arraigned against my father."

Put it down to bad timing. For when Ramesh Chandra was

in the throes of his battle with his father and his uncle, Arjun Singh returned as CM of MP.

It was harrowing when the politician used the powers of his government and locked up the Gwalior printing press and office, under the pretext that it was disputed property.

The ensuing four months were pure hell.

Girish, who was by his father's side in Gwalior while Sudhir took care of Bhopal and Indore, narrated how they stood up to and faced those distressful times.

Incidentally, Girish had been put in charge of the Gwalior office when he was still a schoolboy studying in Class 12.

"Look at the confidence of my father," flashbacked Girish. "When he sent me to look after the Gwalior office, he never even asked me which school I would be studying in. He simply said, 'Ask your mama (mother's brother) who lives in Gwalior.' Today I can't believe that this was how it happened but at that young age when I was barely 15-16 years of age, I got admission to Central School on my own. My father never once visited my school."

He recalled that when Arjun Singh returned to MP as CM, he took full advantage of their family feuds.

"I may have been very young," said Girish, "but I remember the government locking up our press. How does a newspaper function when its office and press are locked up? That's the time I saw the fighting spirit of my father emerge. He told us, 'The show will go on. If we can't operate from within our premises, we will work from outside. They can't stop that, can they?' So we actually put tables and chairs out in the open and operated from there. He had a tent put up and in the 44-degree heat of Gwalior, the entire staff worked inside the tent with the police all around keeping watch over us.

"I saw a very different personality of my father in those days. I'd always thought of him as docile, as someone who wouldn't ever get angry. He was still not shouting and yelling but he was very firm and resolute. He said, 'Who can evict us from here? We'll work and we'll keep working until we get a stay order from the court.' We went to court against the locking up of our office and got a stay. Until then, we would work in the tent and print our newspaper in Jhansi which was 120 kms away. I used to leave Gwalior at 11pm in a car with all the designed pages for the newspaper, reach Jhansi at 1 am, get the paper printed, leave at 4 am and get back home by 6 am. We did it every night for weeks together to ensure that the paper was printed and distributed without a break in publication."

This episode changed forever the way Girish looked at his father.

"Seeing my father so determined that come what may, we won't let the publication of the paper be suspended even for a day, I realised that nothing was impossible. There is always a way around every problem. You just have to find it.

"To call him fearless would be an understatement. I would sometimes get scared and tell him, 'Papa, look at so many policemen around us.' And he would say, 'What can they do? Put me behind bars? So what's the big deal? I will sleep in jail for one night. We haven't done any wrong, we haven't stolen anything from anyone.'

"The lessons I learnt from his fearlessness and from working in such adverse circumstances, have stood me in good stead all my life. I have literally worked from the street. I was proud of my father, of his stand that he wouldn't bend before anybody under any circumstances or any situation. And of his fight for the right reasons."

Sudhir nodded, "During those four months of the Gwalior fight, it was Girish who was with my parents. Yes, my mother was there too. She would sit next to Papa all day. She was not a business woman but she would sit there and not leave until my father went to bed. And she would wake up before him. They had a very, very strong relationship.

"Bhawna, Pawan and I were alone in Bhopal with one domestic help while Girish was there supporting our parents. In those three to four months, I was running the business in Bhopal because I had been involved in it right from 1983. In 1987, I was given independent charge of running the flagship edition of Indore. In 1988, when I was 21, I launched Raipur. So I was with my father throughout his journey."

Sudhir also shared details of a liquor business that his father owned for a very short while.

"We had a liquor license for Indian-made foreign liquor and we ran that business for about five to six months," Sudhir explained. "Dad's friend, Shanti Prasadji, had set it up with him in Mandu. When I shifted to Indore in 1987, my father told me to manage this one too for a few months.

"In the liquor business, you pay excise to the Government, get the license and the truck goes out. Once in a while they have to conduct a raid, where a certain quantity of liquor is seized and it gets into the news. It happened once with our trucks, it was part of a routine raid, nothing out of the ordinary. But my father was unhappy and uneasy about it. He felt that this was a messy business with cash involved. So, soon after we were raided, he decided to exit the business. He said he did not want people to say that whatever Ramesh Agrawal made in his life came from selling *daru,* liquor.

"Around that time, Kailashpati Kedia was a very big liquor baron in Indore, whose CEO was a man called Raghavan. My father had already spoken to him and told him to take over this business of ours in which we had invested Rs 41-42 lakh. Another dealer named Bhadoria who heard about it, offered to take it on lease for Rs 40 lakh. But my father was adamant that he did not want 'Distillery owned by Ramesh Chandra Agarwal' to exist. He preferred to sell it to Kedia for around Rs 35 lakh. So we sold this business for less than the amount we had invested in it. By then the business would have been worth a couple of crores but my dad was so determined to come out of it that he told me to go right then and finish with it. I still remember that at 10.30 pm, I went to Raghavan's house and gave him the keys to the distillery with my father's message, 'You'll be running this from tomorrow. We will have nothing to do with it as of this moment. All we want is for you to sign the papers ASAP and give them to us.' We gave him the keys before we even got any money from them and of course without waiting for any signatures. We completed all those formalities later. But that's how the Mandu business was sold overnight."

It was Ramesh Chandra's desire to involve himself in businesses which worked towards serving society in a positive way that egged him to quit the brewery business without a moment's delay.

Sudhir remembered another incident that happened during the Gwalior stand-off. "Somebody from the Government told me that all my calls were being tapped and that our cars were being followed. He said, 'Something rough is going on in Gwalior and you are fighting with the Government. So all your actions, all your movements in Bhopal are being watched. Be careful.' Then somebody else told me, 'Maybe all your bank accounts will be frozen. What they've done in Gwalior, they might do in Bhopal.' Another person told me, '*Yaar*, it's nothing. It's only an ego clash. Why don't you ask Rameshji to go and talk to the Chief Minister, apologise to him and settle it?' So I called my father in Gwalior and asked him to come down to Bhopal for a discussion. He came and he said, 'If you guys are scared and you want to, then do it. But I don't want to.' He used one line that went, '*Mujhse meri niyati aur kismat koi nahi chheen sakta.* Nobody can take my destiny away from me.' He was absolutely clear that he wouldn't go and apologise or compromise. He believed that if you give in once, it will set a precedent, they will make you dance to their tune all through your life. And that's something he was unwilling to do. He told me, 'It makes no difference to me. I used to stay in a *barsaati,* in one room on the terrace. What can happen to us? At the most we'll have to go back to staying in the *barsaati* and start life all over again. I'm prepared to do that. But you guys decide.'

"So my father never went to meet Arjun Singh. He went back to Gwalior the same night and he fought it out legally. He fought against the entire government machinery, got a stay order from the High Court and got the office re-opened."

The tension between Arjun Singh and Ramesh Chandra Agarwal did ease after a while.

"Yes, when everything was normal, my father met him to say, 'I have nothing against you personally.' He cleared up whatever misunderstanding existed between them."

Congress strongman and current Chief Minister of Madhya Pradesh, Kamal Nath was one of the politicians who counted Ramesh Chandra as a close, personal friend, and was witness to the deadlock between DB and the CM.

He put on record, "I met Rameshji in the early 1980s and was very moved and impressed by his doggedness, determination and vision to spread himself in the media world. DB was not his business, it was his passion. The media sometimes rubs people the wrong way. Our government came into power in Madhya Pradesh in June 1980 and there were times when it didn't like being criticised. So he used to have problems and I became the bridge between our leadership and him. I was close to Arjun Singh also, so I could talk to him about it.

"There came a point when there was a complete breakdown of relations," he recalled. "How do you provide convergence in such a situation?"

Although DB was not a big player then, the animosity between Arjun Singh and Ramesh Chandra, "Came to the notice of even Mrs Indira Gandhi who one day asked me, 'What is this problem between *Dainik Bhaskar* and Mr Arjun Singh?' She was not very familiar with *Bhaskar*. But when I told her that, well, there were problems, she said, 'We must iron them out.'"

Kamal Nath reiterated, "He had serious problems with the Chief Minister and I was the bridge who counselled Arjun Singhji. In the process, I became friendly with Rameshji. What I liked about him was that he was very upright, there was no subterfuge about him.

"After the 1984 Bhopal Gas Tragedy (when Mrs Gandhi was no more and Rajiv Gandhi was in the saddle), DB was very critical of us. Arjun Singh was very upset with them. We were running into an election soon after, the Parliamentary election."

That was the time Rajiv Gandhi pulled Arjun Singh out of Madhya Pradesh and sent him to Punjab as Governor.

Kamal Nath noted, "When this happened, Rameshji remarked, *hamay bahut relief mili hai,* I'm immensely relieved with this."

He also recalled that Ramesh Chandra had a sense of humour. "He could make fun of himself and of others. When Arjun Singh went to Punjab, Rameshji told me, '*Unko wahin rakhiyega.* Singh *naam hai toh Sardar sochenge Sardar hi hai* (Keep him there. With a surname like Singh, the Sardars will think he is one of them).' He would say things like that as a joke."

But time was the eternal healer.

Kamal Nath who had witnessed the meteoric rise of DB from nowhere to right up there, commented, "No newspaper can run unless it's financially viable. Viability is important. You're not going to sell your wife's jewellery to run your newspaper. As long as you run on profit, it's fine. You cannot profiteer. Rameshji knew the difference. So he was essentially a newspaperman. He also foresaw the fact that a good newspaper needs a strong distribution network too. That was his strength and it gave DB an edge over its competitors."

Meanwhile, Ramesh Chandra's gladiatorial court case with his belligerent family stretched on for five years and was settled only in 1992.

Congress party stalwart and former Chief Minister of Madhya Pradesh, Digvijaya Singh was one of the few who knew both father and son and was thus in a position to try and broker peace between them.

"Ramesh Chandra Agarwal belonged to a family which was quite well-known in Gwalior, the area I come from," stated the senior politician.

"I came into contact with Dwarkaji soon after I joined politics in 1971. And I met Rameshji a little later in the 1980s. We were of the same age, so we interacted quite a bit and would often discuss politics. In the 1980s, I became a minister in the state cabinet.

"I always had a free and frank relationship with Rameshji. He had the habit of saying what he wanted to say, he never pulled his punches. That relationship continued till the very end. I've had dinner in his house many a time. I have attended the marriages of all his three sons. I can say that Rameshji's and my relationship was more like that of family friends than that of a journalist and a politician. I'm very happy to say Sudhir, Girish and Pawan have maintained the same relationship with me."

Having known both Dwarka Prasad and Ramesh Chandra closely, Digvijaya Singh was able to see the difference in father and son.

"Both men were very genial, very likeable. But yes, there were problems between them, like there are in many a family.

"Dwarkaji was more of a businessman. He was the one who launched *Dainik Bhaskar*. At that time, it was not like what it is today. It had a small circulation, was more of a tabloid. The credit goes to Rameshji for giving *Bhaskar* a new format and making it really big. Then Sudhir expanded it and took it to a different level altogether," he observed, giving credence to the belief that one of Ramesh Chandra's biggest assets was his trio of sons who bolstered him and made a major contribution to his success story.

But what made Ramesh Chandra's climb even more incredible was that he had to, at several rungs, contend with differences within the family too. And, despite the arduousness of the journey, he still emitted his natural graciousness. Vishambhar's son Manmohan Agarwal's voice broke, overwhelmed with emotion at the memory of his cousin Ramesh Chandra's heart-tugging gestures.

During a phase when the two families were not on cordial terms, Manmohan's sister was getting married. At that time, there was a 100-acre piece of land that the families jointly owned. "Rameshji met my father at a function and he said, 'If we're getting a good price for that land, why don't we sell it?' There was an offer of Rs 18 lakh for it and I needed money at that time. The buyer was giving nine lakh right then and the remaining nine lakh later. I said, 'We'll take four-and-a-half each right now' but Rameshji knew I needed the money. So he had the big heart to give me the entire amount of nine lakh that we first got from the buyer. I can't ever forget that act of kindness by him," Manmohan said.

Once the intra-family squabbles with Vishambhar Dayal were settled in 1992, the DB growth story soared.

"When I look back, what I see is a very gutsy man," said Sudhir. "That was my father's biggest ace and close to that quality was the tremendous faith he reposed in people.

"When we decided to move out of the old Bhopal house, I was a little more than 16 years old. I was the one who got our first bungalow on rent; my father never even saw it before we shifted in. I paid a huge rent for it in those days because I was desperate to move out and go to a proper house. My father gave me *carte blanche* to get it done.

"My grandfather had an Ambassador car and he bought a Fiat from somebody. My father had no interest in personal acquisitions, so when the Maruti was launched and I told my grandfather that I wanted one, he said, '*Theek hai,* go ahead.' And I bought my first car. But my father never once told me, 'Hey, what do you think you're doing?'

"I was very fond of cars. From 1983 onwards, I would go to the State Trading Corporation in Delhi every third month when they would ask for tenders for imported cars. I couldn't afford to buy any at the time but I liked looking around. In 1985, I put in a tender of Rs 1 lakh and got myself a Blue Datsun. My father was fine with it though he never drove it."

Both Sudhir and Girish looked back with amazement that they were mere teenagers when the former expressed a desire to build a swank, imposing office in Bhopal. Ramesh Chandra green-signalled it and didn't once look at even the blueprint, implicitly trusting Sudhir to put up a structure that would inspire awe in the city.

"In 1987, when we made our Bhopal office, which is still our head office, *India Today* did a story on us saying that it was one of the best newspaper offices in the country," Girish stated, feeling rather good about it. "People started wondering how a small newspaper could construct such a spectacular office. But all that my father said to my brother was, 'When you make something, go all out and make it the best.'"

It was the same faith that had urged Ramesh Chandra to hand over the reins of the Indore edition, their biggest at that time, to Sudhir who was not even 20 years old in 1987. Sudhir lived alone in a house in Indore with one domestic help and a car at his disposal. His father trustingly left him to run the Indore end of the business.

Girish who was sent to manage the office in Gwalior when he was still a school kid, also tipped his hat at the manner in which his father had handled family issues.

"My father was not the sort who'd rave and rant but he was very clear in spelling out anything that he felt was wrong. He wouldn't stick around saying 'Yes' to his father simply because he was the breadwinner of the family.

"Once I started seeing how hard he worked on the Indore edition, going back and forth, saw what he was going through and the conviction with which he handled family issues, I came to admire him for the man he was. From an entrepreneur's perspective, my father was a man who could take risks and delegate responsibility. When Bhai (Sudhir) was around 19 years old, Papa sent him to London to visit the machinery fair and select a machine for the press. He put his full faith in such a young person."

Pawan and Bhawna were kids and were largely insulated from the wars at the workplace and the battles within the *parivaar*. But Bhawna recalled that however bitter the battle, family traditions had to be upheld.

"So, while the fight was on, even if we met my uncle or aunt in the market or anywhere else, we couldn't disrespect them and just walk away," she said. "We had to touch their feet and accord complete respect to them, meet them with respect. We were told by our parents that the fight was in the office and it didn't give us the right to be disrespectful to any of the elders in the family. They didn't even discuss these matters in front of us. We would only overhear something once in a while."

There was another interesting incident that Bhawna recalled when Ramesh Chandra put a protective arm around his natural mother and stood tall against his father. It made his mother Kasturi Devi believe even more strongly that her son was Lord Hanuman's gift to her. (Hanuman or the Monkey God, Lord Rama's most loyal devotee, is worshipped for his extraordinary strength, his limitless courage and unflinching devotion.)

"My Dadi (grandmother) was of the firm belief that she got Papa only because of Hanumanji," disclosed Bhawna. "She had gone through a few miscarriages and after praying fervently to

Hanumanji, Papa was born to her. So she always believed that he came into this world with His blessings."

It had to be an extraordinarily powerful blessing for Ramesh Chandra Agarwal to do what he did in 1996.

Chapter 3

DESERT SAFARI

'If I had eight hours to chop down a tree, I'd spend six hours sharpening my axe'

– Abraham Lincoln

Prepping thoroughly came so naturally to Ramesh Chandra that he didn't need to take a leaf out of Lincoln's book. What was also second nature to him was to seek fresh avenues of excitement which was evident when DB was launched in one ambitious market after another, challenging and outrunning the reigning king at every stop. It was one unremitting series of launches, barely stopping to catch their breath before they were off again, chasing another rainbow and finding a pot of gold at the end of the arc.

Archimedes found it in the bathtub. Ramesh Chandra and his sons found their eureka moment amidst sand dunes and camels and men famous for their valour – in Jaipur, Rajasthan, the state known for its magnificent palaces and vibrant pageantry.

In 1995, an audacious idea took birth in Ramesh Chandra's mind and took concrete shape when plans were conceived for a forward step across the state border where the venerable *Rajasthan Patrika* had held sway without any competitor in sight. Initially, the intent was to comfortably ensconce itself in the second place. *Patrika* sold over 1 lakh copies in Jaipur. DB aspired for a circulation of about 50,000, which would snugly place it one rung below *Patrika.* It was a position from where a fairly attractive revenue could be mopped up as the No. 2 newspaper.

With the flair of a seasoned roulette player, Ramesh Chandra took all that he had earned in Madhya Pradesh, a sum that was in the region of Rs 5 crore, and placed it all on Jaipur. He didn't spare a thought to keeping aside a nest egg, he invested it all right back into his business. And business right now was in Jaipur.

But his horizon stretched without boundary as Ramesh Chandra didn't envision Rajasthan as just another market. He glimpsed in it a gigantic opportunity for growth when he bought an expensive piece of land and erected an office building that would stun Jaipur.

It was euphoric when his modestly-estimated 50,000 copies magically and sharply moved North, the needle pointing at an inconceivable figure of 1 lakh, crossing it and settling at the startling starting point of 1.70 lakh copies on its debut day. It was the stuff that fairy tales were made of as the game-plan of starting as No. 2 was left way behind with *Bhaskar* outstripping the circulation of the reigning master to become No. 1 on Day 1.

This rapturous moment came wrapped with many firsts in the world of newspapers. No newspaper had ever launched a door-to-door survey and readers contact programme on such a massive and intensive scale. Nobody in the news dissipation business had done such a survey to understand what the reader wanted and then gone back to take bookings of a paper that had not had even its first print run.

A brilliant thought had driven it. Daewoo had just launched Cielo, their new car in the Indian market and buyers had paid an advance of Rs 50,000 to book it. The bulb in Ramesh Chandra's brain flashed as he asked himself the question, 'If people are willing to pay 50,000 in advance for a car they haven't even seen, why can't we ask for bookings for a newspaper that is still to be printed?' It was an unprecedented move but that was DB's strong suit—to do what nobody had thought of.

It was also the first time that a regional newspaper was being brought out in colour in Rajasthan. It was the first time that a daily was designed on readers' inputs and not by desk-bound editors. Editorially too, it was the first time a vernacular newspaper dispensed with writing numbers in that language and began to write numerals in English. It established a pattern that other publications soon followed.

Ramesh Chandra's first step out of home territory was therefore pathbreaking not only for DB but a trendsetting exemplar for the vast newspaper industry.

But to get there, he and his sons had to undertake a journey that was fraught with perils lurking around every corner. It was the biggest gamble of Ramesh Chandra's life, one which required the nerves of a professional punter. He had to roll the dice and be ready for it to take him back to the bottom of the board like in a snakes and ladders game.

To play outside Madhya Pradesh, he had to go back to being a non-entity, start from scratch, risk it all and in the eventuality of a drubbing, be prepared to even lose it all. But Ramesh Chandra's incurable itch for a new combat needed to be soothed.

"Papa would always say, '*Bahut badiya, achchi mehnat ki tum logo ne, shabash* (Great work, boys, congratulations). *Ab batao,* what next?' We could never put our feet up and relax once a job was done, we were always in the 'what next' mode," laughed Girish.

After facing *Nai Duniya* in its own lair, when the 'what next' landed them in Rajasthan, in keeping with the spirit of the state, the entry of DB had all the elements of colourful palace intrigue: politics, dirty tricks, big bucks and dare-devil heroics.

Before even stepping into what was virgin territory for DB, and throwing a challenge to *Rajasthan Patrika,* the preening No. 1 newspaper of the state, what was required was a therapeutic cleansing and conditioning of the mind. DB had to first accept that it may be a challenger but it was also a nobody in this new terrain.

"For my father to become humble and to start all over again was as instant and easy as the snap of a finger," remarked Sudhir.

"When he went to Rajasthan, he was happy to start from the bottom. He didn't even stop to think that he was a leader in the Madhya Pradesh newspaper industry, the uncrowned king where the Chief Minister came to dine at his place. How could a man as big as he was, go to Rajasthan where he was a nobody? It meant going back to zero. But he didn't even give it a thought. He was excited to start from the bottom and start building again.

"We attained the Numero Uno position in Jaipur, Rajasthan and created world history in the newspaper business. After that, we went to Chandigarh and Haryana, again starting from the bottom. Here too, we started our operations from a tent because our building was still under construction. But he never had a problem, never sought the comforts he was used to or insisted on security guards for himself. Never.

"I think that kept us humble," he analysed, pointing to what made Ramesh Chandra and his three sons, men without arrogance. "We kept doing something again and again from the ground. When you go to an unknown territory you have to start humble."

After establishing DB in Madhya Pradesh, Ramesh Chandra could have taken the easy option of staying put, consolidating his position and enjoy being the undisputed maharaja. But the more thrilling alternative was to move forward and look for new territories to conquer. Much thought was expended on which direction to make the next big leap. Bihar with its low per capita income in the 1990s was not an exciting business proposition (although he did go there as well a little later). Uttar Pradesh already had three players in the fray, *Dainik Jagran*, *Amar Ujala* and *Aaj*.

After learning vital lessons from his experience in Indore, when he put a foot into Jaipur to jostle for space alongside *Rajasthan Patrika*, he came fully armed for battle.

He stepped over the border and chose Rajasthan as the first state outside Madhya Pradesh for hoisting the DB flag for a bunch of reasons. It was once the home state of his ancestors; one that was bordering his comfort zone of MP. Besides cultural similarity; there was only one major competitor here. So even if DB occupied the second slot, it was still a good enough position to generate healthy ad revenue. Rajasthan was also a commercially rich, growing state and most of all, Hindi—the language that ticked in the Agarwal heart with pride—was read and understood all over this sparkling state.

But there was also a rumour that he was piggybacking on a powerful political entity and had been invited to breach the bastion of *Patrika* which seemed to be leaning towards another ideology. The scenario was a repeat of *l'affaire Nai Duniya* whose political leanings had opened a window for DB.

In Rajasthan, BJP stalwart Bhairon Singh Shekhawat was the Chief Minister.

Chief Election Commissioner Sunil Arora who was then Secretary to the CM of Rajasthan, had met Ramesh Chandra, "Sometime in 1995 when he had come to Jaipur to meet Late Bhairon Singhji and unveil his plans to set up DB in Rajasthan.

"*Rajasthan Patrika* had been there for a very long time," he remembered. "Two other Hindi papers, *Dainik Navjyoti* and

Rashtradoot were also based in Rajasthan. At one point of time Rameshji's family had links with the state but had later put down roots in MP. When he set foot in Rajasthan, everybody had heard about *Bhaskar*, it was not an unknown entity," he added.

From meeting at the office to often catching up at Arora's home, becoming personal family friends was a natural step forward for the two gentlemen. But the retired IAS officer recalled what made Ramesh Chandra stand out in the crowd.

"What struck me was that he came to Rajasthan with all the sums and calculations done in his head. A gentleman who was in charge of his marketing for a long time would invariably accompany him. Rameshji was very thorough. Over a period of time, we found they had also done their own research with advance teams and had come fully prepared.

"I was then Secretary to the CM and also held the position of Secretary Information of Rajasthan. It was my job to do the hand holding," Arora explained. "Those days he would mostly wear his trademark off-white safari suit," he casually added.

'Hand holding' took the form of being the centrepoint between a determined new entrant who knew the rules of the game and was prepared to play it to his full capacity and a Chief Minister who was pleased with the editorial performance of *Rajasthan Patrika* and therefore, unwilling to entertain the media house of another state.

"Rameshji faced all kinds of covert opposition," Arora stated candidly. "I was told that there were attempts to delay the recognition the state gives for the release of advertisements. Attempts by certain quarters," he alleged. And the CM was playing ball with 'certain quarters'.

"I told the CM one day, 'With due regards, what can you do? You can perhaps delay it by a maximum of six months. But after six months, the rates will get automatically approved.' DAVP (Directorate of Advertising & Visual Publicity which released ads) was in any case not a state body, it was a part of the I&B

Ministry. I told the CM that when such a big player was coming here, already established with impeccable credentials, we should in fact be going all out to assist him and not create imaginary roadblocks.' Because my own perception was that the roadblocks were completely imaginary.

"Shekhawatji was initially misled by vested interests who gave him prejudiced, non-objective feedback," he presented the insider's view. "Rameshji was too decent to mention that initially it was one of Shekhawatji's advisers—one who is no more so I wouldn't like to name him—who was playing both sides. Telling the other guys, these people have come because they've been brought in by some very big political person."

With such strong political opposition by no less an authority than the Chief Minister of the state, what made Ramesh Chandra enter Rajasthan and face the bodyline googlies, was analysed by Arora. He said, "Rameshji had once told me that they had the capacity to bear initial losses. He knew all the tricks of the trade and had even created his own band and team of dedicated hawkers. This was before the digital era when hawkers were the backbone of the distribution network. They started a) selling the newspaper at a lower rate and b) charging less for advertisements. They were prepared to wage battle, so they were bound to win. And they won. I had no doubt from Day 1 that it made better sense to go along with them than to oppose them."

Editorially, DB did the opposite of the more pliant *Patrika*—they took on Shekhawat. Yet, Ramesh Chandra was innately a PR man, so despite the editorial aggression, he knew how to smoothen out the creases.

"He was very polite and would always be sizing up the milieu around," Arora said. "The family, they all have core strengths. They developed their niche areas and niche domain knowledge about various provinces.

"Subsequently, one of his sons got married into a very

prominent and illustrious family in Rajasthan. So a personal relationship also got established," he cannily remarked.

By the time they set foot in Rajasthan, Sudhir was already married to Jyoti (they wed in 1993). Interestingly, Ramesh Chandra's adventures in two places outside his home state brought two fine daughters-in-law into the family. Much later, when he would venture towards Chandigarh, Ramesh would find a bride for his youngest son Pawan there. In Rajasthan, while DB found a discreet supporter in business tycoon SK Golcha, the association also ushered bliss into Girish's personal life when he found a warm and companionable wife in Namita Golcha.

One of the most respected names of Jaipur, SK Golcha traced his association with *Patrika* and the subsequent transfer of his affection to DB.

"I was once associated with *Patrika*," he said with candour. "My father had helped set it up from our *haveli* in the old city in the late 1950s. It broke all records and overtook *Rashtradoot* which was the reigning paper then. But later, there was a rift between Kulishji (Karpoor Chandra Kulish of *Patrika*) and my father and we parted. *Patrika* was one-sided, they tended to give only the BJP-Jan Sangh point of view. In fact, that was the conflict between my father and Kolsiji. When I met Girish and Sudhir, I asked them, 'Can you overtake *Patrika*?' They very modestly said, 'Uncle, we're trying. Can you help us find some land?'

"I told them that if you start DB here, you should be prepared to face losses for the first five years. But that thought was overturned by the two who exceeded expectations when they shook up everybody in the first year itself," he noted admiringly. "I didn't know they would take on *Patrika* so strongly, the way they marketed *Bhaskar* aggressively, it created history."

The DB team, flush with the adrenaline rush of battle, had a blueprint for a multi-pronged attack on the fortress of *Patrika*.

But the most appreciable element in the battle was that it was constructive and positive—there was no negative thrust against their opponent, however daunting the challenge.

The ground reality was that the Jaipur edition of *Rajasthan Patrika* was selling around 1.4 lakh copies in Jaipur. *Patrika's* nearest rival *Navjyoti* was a far second with a figure of approximately 25,000 copies.

Compelling lessons learnt from their Indore experience came into play in Rajasthan. Indore had been a traditional battle where they found solutions to problems as and when they arose.

Rajasthan was meticulously planned and fought with the core team strategising its moves with accuracy and secrecy. When celebrity writer Kamleshwar was brought on board as Editor but was too busy to be available in Jaipur more than once or twice a week, dependable Shravan Garg took on the editorial responsibilities which included sending staffers from MP to Rajasthan and recruiting new talent.

At home, the family made its key decisions at the breakfast table which had turned into a private board room. A charming sidelight was that the Agarwals shifted *en famille* to Jaipur to provide the support system for 'the boys'. Mario Puzo famously said, 'The strength of a family, like the strength of an army, is in its loyalty to each other.' The move *en masse* to Jaipur set a precedent and became tradition for the family to set up temporary residence whenever DB entered a new state. Every major launch thus because a family affair where everybody pitched in to make a healthy contribution.

It was an exhilarating time for the entire DB *parivaar* as the team was on an inexpressible high, meeting unforeseen challenges, foregoing sleep and compromising with creature comforts.

A house was rented in Jaipur and it operated like a hotel-cum-hostel for the team that worked for 18 to 20 hours a day for months. Tension was high, the schedule punishing with no question of a break as one formidable task after the other loomed large and had to be tackled on a war footing. Portfolios and designations were blurred as every member rolled up his shirt sleeves and put his nose to the grind.

Food came in tiffin boxes for the whole team and Girish, always the great organiser, would distribute Jaipur's famous sweets to everybody. Pawan would turn his luxury car into a mini-bus, drop off the team at the hotel-hostel and then head home to catch 40 winks. It was high-spirited camaraderie brought about by soldiering together for what seemed like an impossible fantasy.

Sanjay Jain, Vice-President DB Malls & Hotel Business, started his exhilarating journey with Ramesh Chandra in Jaipur.

"It's an experience that still stays with me," he enthused, reliving the euphoric weeks. "It was sheer energy, difficult to explain. Everybody was bound together by a single rope that was moving on a very high plane.

"I'm a Chartered Accountant, I'd been hired for accounts and finance. But given the kind of momentum that had set in, everybody was available to run around and do everything, irrespective of which department they belonged to."

Strategy, brainwork and elbow grease of a very high order combined to pull it off. The employer-employee line ceased to exist as Sudhir, Girish and Pawan slogged alongside their staff. On a couple of nights, Pawan would simply curl up on the pile of waste paper and go to sleep.

But tension was always around the corner.

It began at the very basic level of acquiring land for their office building.

"Papa could never think small," recalled Sudhir Agarwal, the business and editorial brain of DB.

"We were looking for land in Jaipur and I had hired Mr

Menon, a UNI Bureau Chief, to find us something appropriate. He called me one day and said, 'Sudhir, I've got a piece of land in Jaipur.' I said, 'Great, how much?' He said, 'Rs 84 lakh. The government price is 21, but it's being given to us at the commercial price of 84.'

"I told my father, Rs 84 lakh is too high a price for land that's on the outskirts of Jaipur. But he said, 'Nothing doing. It is a good, 1-acre land, just take it.' He was so determined, he told me to make a bank draft, take a train and personally go deposit the money."

Once again, Ramesh Chandra had a clear mandate for Sudhir to send out a message so strong that all of Jaipur would know who had arrived in their city. *Patrika* had a sprawling building like a grand old fort. Ramesh Chandra told Sudhir, 'Don't create something inconsequential that will give the impression that an effete player has come to Jaipur. Make the kind of building that will make people sit up and notice it and feel that a strong and substantial contender has entered the arena.'"

The grand building that Sudhir erected did herald the entry of a muscular challenger.

But earlier, when Sudhir had reached the office of the Jaipur Development Authority to deposit Rs 84 lakh for buying the land, the officer concerned had mocked him. He was told jeeringly that the land was being allotted only for a newspaper and that it would be impossible to sell it commercially in Jaipur. The message was unequivocal that they'd be better off retracing their steps back to where they came from.

The JDA officer was one among the many who offered the Agarwals the same two-word advice: go home. But Ramesh Chandra had done his homework, he had come battle-equipped with deep pockets that he was willing to dip into and spend. He wanted to make a majestic entry, no matter what the cost, as he firmly believed that regional newspapers were treated shabbily because they were considered to be 'petty-minded'. As Sudhir said, he thought big. He not only purchased prime land in Jaipur at four times the government price which was like a calling card being presented to the Shekhawat regime and *Patrika* but also hired Indore's famous architect Achal Chaudhary to put up an awe-inspiring edifice within six months.

While the building was still under construction, Girish road-mapped a pathbreaking marketing programme and Pawan carried out a large-scale survey of the readership they were out to woo.

It was during the Jaipur adventure that the Chief Technology Officer (CTO) and indispensable member of the DB core team, RD Bhatnagar was dramatically inducted into the company.

22 years later, he recalled it with the relish of a recent happening.

RD was with *The Times Of India* when one fine morning, "I got a call from Raja, one of my colleagues who had joined DB. He told me straightaway that Mr Sudhir Agarwal would be calling me. I didn't know who that was."

RD had no inkling that the Sudhir he was clueless about was going to become an integral part of his life, for the rest of his life.

"When Mr Sudhir Agarwal called me and started speaking to me, I was in a fix. I did not know the person on the other end of the phone line," he said, merriment still playing on his face. "Then he introduced himself and said, 'We will be coming out with our newspaper *Dainik Bhaskar* and since you have been working in Jaipur, we want to understand the market there.' I had been with TOI in Jaipur for about five years."

But RD was in Delhi that day.

"The most dramatic part was when Raja said, 'Mr Agarwal is going to send you a ticket. Why don't you come to Jaipur the day after tomorrow?' I said, I can't leave so early, but he said, 'Just try and manage, it's a Saturday.' The very next morning, I got a ticket for the Shatabdi Express from Delhi to Jaipur which got me acquainted with the speed at which they worked. I took the ticket, caught the train, came to Jaipur and reached the address pretty early by about 10.30 am. I went to the half-constructed basement which was the only part of the building that had been made so far. One machine had been installed there and there were a couple of people moving around. I was standing there when a gentleman in a bush shirt with his sleeves rolled up came up and asked me who I was looking for. I told him, 'I am looking for Mr Sudhir Agarwal' and he said, 'Okay, come in.' We went into one of the rooms and he sat across the table," he chuckled, still delighted that the MD himself had so casually sauntered across to him.

"While we were talking, another simply dressed gentleman who looked slightly older than Sudhirji, walked in, took a seat nearby and said, 'Keep talking'. I didn't know who he was. It was only when I was walking away that I heard Sudhirji address the other gentleman as 'Papa'. That was when I realised he was his father but I still didn't know that he was the Chairman of the organisation. Such a simple man. I'd been brought up at TOI where we never saw Ashokji (Ashok Jain), the Chairman. Ashokji used to sit in the same building on Bahadur Shah Zafar Marg but for 30 to 35 years he'd never gone down the stairs to the machine room. And here was the Chairman of DB actually sitting in a half-constructed building, standing near the machine. It was a very different experience.

"The Jaipur launch was one of the most interesting, most fabulous, most challenging times that I've had in my entire career," he rhapsodised. "That was when DB actually took off. It took off on a vertical flight. It was no more a plane, it was a rocket and I was one of the crew members. Really, even today I cherish the moment I took the decision to join DB."

While Sudhir hired staff and crunched numbers with his father, Girish was in natural flow in the marketing department.

The teaser-hoarding which announced the arrival of DB in Rajasthan declared, 'Now, the sun will rise from the west in the skies of Jaipur'. It may have been puzzling, even amusing, but implicit in the statement was that the impossible was going to happen. It certainly succeeded in upping the curiosity of Jaipur.

The Jaipur launch broke many traditions. Conventionally, a newspaper would be launched, its readership assiduously built and then it would be marketed. But DB turned this wisdom on its head. Its office building was still in its bricks-and-cement stage, the launch was months away, but the marketing had begun. And that too, with a quizzical statement which was followed by hoardings carrying a fresh message every 10 days.

It was carpet bombing by the marketing team. More than two lakh pamphlets were delivered door-to-door along with the local newspapers. Camels and elephants with banners of DB strung on them started making rounds of the city. Once the name *Dainik Bhaskar* began to ring with familiarity, the next step was to make direct contact with the people through a readership survey. Sudhir explained, "Papa wanted to know, what do the people of Jaipur want? What kind of newspaper do they wish to read? What do they think about the newspaper they are currently reading? Does it come up to their expectations? If not, what is missing in it?"

The campaign was christened, 'A newspaper of the readers, for the readers, by the readers'. Another departure from norm was that the survey was conducted by an in-house team since Ramesh Chandra and his sons felt that outside agencies tended to conduct only sample surveys, interacting with a limited number of people and making projections on that basis. While this could work in a First World country where people were homogenous in terms of their educational and social backgrounds, India had wide differences in education, social patterns, standard of living and habits. Also, challenges and niggling areas would be sugar coated by agencies, thus presenting a rosy but not factual picture.

The survey by the home team was not only an important component of the Jaipur plan, it was also the launch pad for Pawan Agarwal, Director DB Corp, who had freshly graduated from Purdue University in the US and was raring to go.

"My dad and brothers inducted me into the company with the launch of Jaipur," he recalled enthusiastically.

"It was my first experience, all four of us were involved in it and this gave me a big high. I was just 21 years old and had not led a team of even two until then, and here, Papa gave me a team of 275 people. He gave me the opportunity and had the faith that I could lead them."

Pawan was so motivated that he happily worked, "18 hours a day from 6 am to sometimes even past midnight."

In the under-construction part of the building, while labourers hurried around with shovels and spades, 275 young surveyors donning the cap and T-shirt of *Bhaskar* got ready to set out and meet the people of Jaipur. Before they stepped into the field, they were given practical training, told what their objective was and how to achieve it. They were also told how to dress, how to carry themselves and how to greet the person who opened the door. During the training sessions, Pawan moved among the surveyors, pointing out if someone had unkempt hair, was unshaven or was wearing unpolished shoes.

To get a first-hand feel of the ground situation, Pawan himself wore the *Bhaskar* Tee and cap and rang the bell of many a Jaipur resident. Many a time, he was shooed away too but the experience he gained was useful for the team and for drawing conclusions from the survey.

"Papa told me," said Pawan, "Go and meet every single person in the city, look for homes that have cemented brick walls, or a gas connection, check out whether their homes have been electrified. Those are the houses to be interested in."

Determined to succeed, in 54 working days between 18 August and 16 October 1996, the surveyors completed the first round of survey of more than two lakh families. Pawan who had studied the psyche of a resident who opens the door to an unknown person, knew that going empty-handed would not be a wise move. "So we sent a gift for the readers every time our team members met them," Pawan disclosed their strategy. "At the first meeting, they presented a 'Jaipur Handbook' to the residents of the city. It contained a map of Jaipur, along with useful phone numbers. Coincidentally, the government telephone directory of the city had not been updated for quite a while. Naturally, those who received the handbook preserved it for easy reference."

The surveyors were explicitly instructed not to request the residents to buy the newspaper the first time around. Pawan was clear that the surveyors were not to conduct themselves like salesmen. "The objective of the first visit was to simply greet readers, try to befriend them and generate goodwill for *Bhaskar* by presenting a small gift to them."

Late at night, the information collected by the surveyors was fed into computers and a daily report generated for the top bosses.

The main takeaway from the data was that there was an empty shelf in the market for an objective, unbiased and reasonably priced newspaper.

During his Jaipur debut, Pawan learnt many a lesson on the job with his father pointing him in the right direction.

"One of the first things Papa taught me was, there's no such thing as an average. If I said, 'Today, on an average we met 15 people,' Papa would say, 'Don't talk to me about the average. It's like rice and husk. Separate them and show me the quantity of rice and show me the husk. If you break it down into smaller categories, high performers, mid-performers and low performers, you'll realise which areas you have to work on. Only then will I be able to decipher what the obstacles are and why only some were able to meet 20.'

"It was an enjoyable experience because he made us think.

"Field work brought to my notice that readers also felt their equation with a newspaper was like the one between a *raja* (king) and his *praja* (subjects). Readers didn't feel the ownership of it.

"So our approach was to bring down that barrier, to ask people to tell us, to write in to say what kind of a newspaper they wanted to read. We went all out to be inclusive, *logon ko jodna*, bring people together with us.

"We also realised that a newspaper was not viewed as reading material for the whole family. Women and youngsters wondered, what's in it for us?

"Once we studied the findings of the survey, we went back to the same households and said, 'We have heard you. Now this is what our product will look like, this is the paper we intend to bring out based on your inputs. Will you be our reader from Day 1? Give us a chance. If don't like it, cancel it. If you like it, continue with it.' That was how we launched Jaipur. It was Papa's idea to first bring the people on board with you. Make every reader the owner of the paper. Tell every reader that he has the *adhikaar*, the authority over the paper."

This was the second and last round done by the surveyors who now announced that DB would begin publication from 19 December 1996.

And the response was overwhelming. Jaipur had been awash for months with banners and hoardings, and Bhaskar-sponsored celebrations of every local festival, rounded off with a buzz around the grand building coming up in their midst. It got curiouser and curiouser with Jaipur and its neighbouring areas witnessing the house-to-house connect made by smartly turned out surveyors. The combination yielded such astonishing results that it stunned the Chairman, his sons, the DB *parivaar* and the entire newspaper industry. It shook Jaipur society.

Preparations began for launching the Jaipur edition of DB with a circulation of 1,72,000 copies. It was such an undreamt-of figure that they weren't even fully equipped to handle it.

Unlike the Indore edition which had started off with unimpressive content that needed vast improvement, DB had entered Jaipur like a veteran. The editorial team had its work cut out for it a month before D-Day. Journalists, rookies and veterans, were introduced to the culture of DB. Reporters went out into the field and filed exclusive stories. They had to write and re-write the same story dozens of times until the editors were satisfied with the copy.

But despite the many hours spent on 'sharpening the axe', the team led by Ramesh Chandra had to tackle the monumental, unforeseen complication of matching their machine capacity with the unprecedented booking of orders.

It was best told in CTO RD Bhatnagar's words. "The paid bookings for DB were so phenomenal that we crossed over 1,00,000 subscriptions. The response was far beyond what we had imagined or been prepared for because our printing machine had the capacity to print only 50,000 or a maximum of 75,000 a night. We had a second machine with which we were experimenting a split shift kind of arrangement and it wasn't working out. So we were virtually left with only one machine. I can still recall that my technical team and I were standing on the ramp after lunch when Sudhirji walked up to us followed by Chairmansaab a few paces behind. Before any conversation could start, he asked Sudhirji, 'Now what do we do?' We had already crossed bookings for 1,00,000 copies and with the tempo having picked up tremendously, the order was expected to go beyond 1,50,000 copies which would've been impossible to meet with just two machines.

"In the basement where we were standing, there was place for only two machines. There was a third row which housed all kinds of material from various departments like HR, Finance and Store. The construction was still going on and we had not yet gone beyond the first floor. The Chairman told Sudhirji that we must get a third machine immediately, come what may, from anywhere. The entire team started getting goose bumps. We were on the verge of a launch and here we were talking about getting another machine which would take about 30 to 32 days to install. And where would we put it anyway?

"Within five minutes of this conversation, Sudhirji called up the manufacturer and told him that he didn't care how he would manage it but he wanted one machine of such-and-such configuration immediately. The Printers House (TPH) was a company which always had a machine being manufactured on the floor. It was one of the prime manufacturers at that point of time and Sudhirji knew the owner Mr Kohli who heard him out with astonishment and then queried, 'Are you kidding me? You want a machine to be delivered in a couple of days? It takes months to manufacture one....' But Sudhirji was persistent and he pushed Mr Kohli, 'You must have a machine on the floor for someone else which you can divert to us.' Fortunately, there was a machine which was being custom-built for another newspaper. Sudhirji somehow persuaded him and said, 'Whatever money you want, you will get tomorrow.' I saw it all happen before my own eyes. A machine that was being made for another customer was thus diverted to us. Sanjay Jain left by car the next day for Delhi to personally deliver the Demand Draft to TPH. In no time at all, we had the third machine on the floor."

But they had to still grapple with the baffling question of where to install it and how to do the job in seven days instead of the 30 that a machine normally required to be up and running.

"It was 7.30 pm by the time we took the decision to put it

in the third bay which was full of stuff from other departments. The people who used to sit in those offices had left for the day, the accounts department, the stores and everything was locked. It was winter time in Jaipur. Another team member, Sanjay Jain and I, the daredevils of those times, went to a nearby compound, picked all the hefty labourers from there, told them we'd give them three times what they normally got, went to the market, purchased all the equipment that was required to break the wall because we couldn't bring bulldozers inside, and went to work.

"With hammers, crowbars, chisels and stuff like that, and 40 to 50 labourers with us, we broke the entire ground floor. We dismantled the offices, shifted all the material stored in the third bay to someplace else, and began to dig almost two feet deep to lay the foundation. It needed huge reinforced cement, concrete RCC, to lay a foundation on which the new machine could be installed. When the machine arrived, we had the floor ready for it."

But there was no time to take a deep breath of satisfaction for the print order booking had touched 1,50,000 and still counting, while the machine needed a minimum of 1 month to be properly installed. And the launch was just a week away.

"A lot of pressure was building up on us, so our core team turned into military men. We didn't think of breaking any records, all we had in mind was that on 19 December, the new machine had to be ready to take our entire print order. With military precision, what used to take 32 days was installed in 72 hours flat."

On the day of the inauguration, former Prime Minister Atal Bihari Vajpayee, walked in.

The team held its breath.

"As an inauguration ritual, Atalji pressed the button to start the machine that we had designated for him," Bhatnagar narrated. "He pressed the button and... the paper tore. This was because it had absorbed too much moisture and become weak. The paper snapped and we were in a fix. Putting the paper back and starting afresh would have taken about 15 to 20 minutes. Since it was only a symbolic run, we walked Mr Vajpayee to the new machine which had paper and ink loaded on it, but hadn't been tested at all."

It was a voila moment when the Chief Guest pushed the button and to the amazement of the team that had least expected it to start, the machine whirred into action. And the team collectively exhaled a sigh of relief!

"The reason why I've narrated the whole incident in detail is to illustrate Chairman Sir's mindboggling pace, the way his mind would race," explained RD. "We printed about 1,72,000 copies which was phenomenal, nobody in the trade or anywhere in the country could imagine such a figure. It was almost twice the figure we were printing elsewhere. But even before Jaipur was fully launched, the Chairman's mind had jumped to what next. Within 10-12 days, we were talking about a launch in Ajmer. For the next 10 to 12 years, every six months we were launching an edition here or there."

For Ramesh Chandra, his adventure in the deserts of Rajasthan was particularly satisfying because once again, he was able to break a monopoly that had existed and had been unquestioningly accepted thus far.

Dainik Bhaskar which had crossed the border successfully in December 1996, with its spectacularly successful Jaipur edition, soon became the pick of Rajasthan.

With the lavish splash he made in Rajasthan, Ramesh Chandra demonstrated once again that he was an entrepreneur with a long-term goal and not a trader who balanced his books every night. He had spent in five to six months, what others might have grudgingly spread over five to six years. But, as he told his team, "If we had spent the money over five to six years, we would have got the results also leisurely in five to six years. By taking the risk of spending money at the outset, we got the results in just five to six months."

Managing Editor Jagdish Sharma who joined the team in 1996 to launch the Jaipur edition, encapsulated the Chairman's success story with three quick lessons that he had picked up.

"One of Rameshji's marked qualities was speed. He was quick with decisions. He would say that certain decisions could go wrong. But if five out of 100 decisions were to go wrong, one couldn't sacrifice the benefits of 95 correct decisions fearing the fate of the five that could go wrong.

"His second lesson was, always pay attention to ground realities; if you go by *andaaza* (guesswork, estimation), you will always go wrong. He gave a lot of importance to what the man on the ground felt. Does the person you want to reach out to understand your campaign?

"The third was, be fearless. For instance, when we faced some tough situations in Rajasthan (because of the might of the competitor), some people felt, maybe we should withdraw a bit, soften our stance. But Rameshji's instructions were, keep working, don't be afraid."

It took Ramesh Chandra a decade (1980-1990) to make DB the No. 1 newspaper in his home state of Madhya Pradesh, but only 1 year to do the same in Jaipur. And to think he had put his first foot in with the modest target of occupying only the No. 2 slot.

The fairy-tale rise of DB was succinctly described by *Business India* in its cover story titled 'Making Headlines' in June, 2008. Making a reference to the spectacular Jaipur launch of 1996, the magazine wrote in its editorial, "A little over 11 years ago, a young man came to the *Business India* office excited about the launch of the Jaipur edition of his newspaper. He talked passionately about conducting large-scale surveys asking readers what they wanted in a newspaper. This pre-marketing was a more effective way than advertising, of telling readers that a new paper was about to be launched. Girish Agarwal, the second son of Ramesh Agarwal and the then advertising director, was strongly of the view that the launch merited a much larger story than the one page that *Business India* had allocated. He also confidently argued that, one day, *Business India* would put the Bhaskar Group on the cover.

"Today, Bhaskar well merits a cover story."

But to retrace DB's steps to 1996, as Girish once said about his father, "He was always hungry for more."

There was indeed much more in store.

Chapter 4

No. 1 IN 35 YEARS: 1983-2017

'I don't believe in taking right decisions.
I take decisions and then make them right'

—Ratan Tata

Thus far it had been Hindi vs Hindi—as in *Dainik Bhaskar* vs *Nai Duniya* and *Dainik Bhaskar* vs *Rajasthan Patrika*. However formidable the opponent and however strong his political clout, it was still in the comfort zone of Hindi journalism where Ramesh Chandra launched his major attacks—and became flush with victory. But would a warrior feel like an emperor by vanquishing only venerable figures who spoke his own language?

By the time the DB juggernaut established its supremacy all over Rajasthan, the restive Chairman had hunted down an even bigger challenge. His primary group that had tasted blood, girdled its loins in readiness and itched for a fresh bout in a new arena. But when the new millennium dawned, Ramesh Chandra gave them the high of the unexpected and their addiction to excitement got a booster shot when he named their new battleground: Chandigarh and Haryana.

Chandigarh was the bastion of a club-going upper middle class; an English-reading public that picked up only *The Tribune* that the butler brought in on a tray. Therefore, it was not only about taking on a mighty adversary, it was also about changing the very mindset of the reader and convincing him to switch from an English diet to a desi thali. There was every chance that Chandigarh would sniff snootily and not roll out the red carpet for the Hindiwallah.

Pawan Agarwal commented, "Hurdles and problems never evoked fear in Papa. They only provoked, motivated and energised him."

So far, Ramesh Chandra had only broken the Hindi newspaper world's self-limiting tradition of not challenging an established monopoly. In Indore, Rajasthan, everywhere he went, he gave the Hindi newspaper a newfound respect, forcing it to smarten up physically with better paper, ink and technology and to change its mental makeup as well—to heave its chest and play the game like a champion, and not as a snivelling, shrinking entity killing itself with an inferiority complex. He had infused a new respectability into Hindi newspapers in Madhya Pradesh and Rajasthan as creative and aggressive marketing brought in enough revenue for every *Bhaskar* edition to stand on its own feet and be counted as a major player by advertisers and clients. The spill-over benefited other regional language players as well. The days of wobbling along weakly were relegated to the dustbins of history.

In Chandigarh, Ramesh Chandra upped the ante; he was out to topple a several-decades-old belief that this was not their market. He looked to demolish the Hindi newspaper industry's low self-esteem which had convinced itself that the English-reading, educated North Indian wouldn't touch the Devnagari papers. But the one question that dogged his logical mind and sought an answer was, why would a populace that relished its *parathas* and loved the *bhangra* (the robust dance of Punjab) not read a Hindi newspaper? DB just had to find the right way to a Chandigarh resident's heart, learn how to serve desi fare with liveried style.

As always, Ramesh Chandra put to work his well-oiled twin strategy of an awe-inspiring edifice that would knock the sails off the complacently well-established veterans, and a survey team that was trained to meet and discover the reading habits and desires of Chandigarh which was home to a host of retired civil servants and defence personnel. Special efforts were also put into producing a sophisticated newspaper that would cater to a readership that was used to a touch of style in what it picked up to read.

But the best brainwave that Ramesh Chandra got and pushed for, revolutionised Hindi papers. He told his editorial team that it was time to use popular, colloquial language—Hindi with a few well-used English, Urdu and Punjabi words. Language purists who resisted the change were told that this was a newspaper, not a piece of literature they were producing.

"The biggest *badlaav* (change) that DB brought about in journalism all over the country was that we did not bring out a newspaper in Hindi but in the language that Chandigarhites normally spoke," noted National Editor—*Mobile App,* Navneet Gurjar, who joined DB as a senior sub-editor in 1999. "*Guruvar* (Thursday) became *Veervar* (as the Punjabi preferred to call it). We used to refer to the Collector as *zilladheesh,* but started calling him/her Collector, school was no longer *pathshala,* it became school. *Zilla karyalay* became the Collectorate. We started using normal everyday words like car, train and birthday in our editorial copy. Our writing began mirroring everyday language. The usage of *shudh* Hindi that we had been imposing on readers stopped from the time we launched the Chandigarh edition. In three months, we put this into practice in all our editions."

Thus was born 'Hinglish', the language that went on to become fashionable and began to be used liberally and extensively all over the country.

But Ramesh Chandra and sons didn't take anything for granted.

Dr L Gulati, who was editorial adviser of the Chandigarh edition, pointed to his own appointment as an exemplary indicator of the alertness and alacrity of the DB family. Gulati had settled down in Chandigarh after his retirement when a surveyor from DB visited his house to record his thoughts on what a newspaper should offer and look like. "I casually wrote a very scathing comment on the survey form and forgot all about it," he recalled mirthfully. Much to his surprise, he got a polite call from the *Bhaskar* office the next day, wondering if he could please come by and meet the Managing Director. Gulati was impressed when a car drove up to fetch him and he was received at the DB gate by the surveyor who had met him at home.

"He took me to a gentleman who did not look like an MD in either age or attire," Gulati chuckled. On the MD's table was the survey form with Gulati's comments. Sudhir was straightforward. He told Gulati that DB would appreciate it if he would do an appraisal of the newspaper they intended publishing in Chandigarh to ensure that it catered to the city's culture and didn't offend its residents in any way.

For the first time in the history of Chandigarh, a Hindi newspaper strode into the city as the No. 1 daily.

But Ramesh Chandra was not a man to put his feet up and relax. Just 27 days after the launch of the Chandigarh edition, he went into neighbouring Haryana and launched the Panipat and Hisar editions. Technologically abreast of the best, DB had satellite editions from 13 districts with the installation of computers, modems, generators and other basic equipment in all the newly established district offices.

2,70,000 copies of the Haryana edition—a history-making figure—were published on the first day.

What Ramesh Chandra and the DB family discovered was that each new territory came with its share of quirky uniqueness.

Managing Editor Jagdish Sharma remembered one marked idiosyncrasy of the Haryana launch. "There was no one who knew how to give an advertisement. And not even one district reporter who was a paid employee of the existing newspapers," Sharma detailed the casual approach to newspapers that once existed. Reporters would be hired on a commission basis.

Jagdish had an unbelievable experience when he was hiring staff for the Haryana edition. He himself drove a Maruti 800 those days. So when a luxury car arrived outside his Yamunanagar office, the driver jumped out to open the door and a well suited-booted man strode in, Jagdish was certain that a VIP visitor had come to meet him. His reaction turned to astonishment when he realised that his visitor had arrived to be interviewed for a reporter's job.

One of the reasons Haryana took to DB was because the state which got its independence from Punjab in 1966, had so far lived in the shadow of its earlier name. Newspapers would be published from Chandigarh or Punjab but nobody gave Haryana a paper of its own. DB went the whole hog to give Haryana its very own identity by publishing editions from 12 of its districts. Along with DB would go a *Rohtak Bhaskar* or a *Panipat Bhaskar* or a *Kurukshetra Bhaskar*. Haryana was no longer going to be clubbed with Punjab.

But it was time to move again. On two battlefronts, Ramesh Chandra had tasted victory: Hindi vs Hindi (MP, Rajasthan) and Hindi vs English (Chandigarh). The magnitude of the new challenge had to match his entrepreneurial appetite. The year 2001 was a fallow year when newsprint prices had shot up steeply and disturbed the newspaper industry to such an extent that even Ramesh Chandra didn't ask the question, "What next?"

In 2002, with Bhawna getting married in April and Pawan in June, Ramesh Chandra and sons diverted all their attention to the two big family events.

"But after two years of not challenging ourselves again, a new market had started brewing in Papa's mind," Sudhir said. "He told us, 'We've already got a presence in various Hindi markets. To be a big player we need to look at a wider, stronger market. We should look at Gujarat.' We didn't consider UP because it wasn't growing at that time and it was also a three-player market. So Gujarat was the market for us. To those who said we would be outsiders there, our standard reply was that the territory didn't worry us. We had already been to Chandigarh, Haryana and Rajasthan. As for the writing, content would be written by professional journalists familiar with the local language and not by us. Papa would also joke that Rupert Murdoch didn't know Hindi when he launched Star TV, the biggest GEC in India.

"However, when Papa conceived the idea of Gujarat he was unaware that the rest of us were going through an emotional disturbance on the family front," Sudhir disclosed. "My mother was very unwell but we hadn't divulged all the details of her illness to my father. By September 2002, when he mentioned Gujarat to us, we were already dealing with my mother's illness, so our response to him was uncharacteristically weak. Papa must have wondered why we were not jumping into it with our usual enthusiasm. We were in a dilemma and weren't sure how to react to his Gujarat plans.

"So we had an internal family chat amongst ourselves without Papa and decided that if we continued to be unenthusiastic, he would wonder what was wrong. Mummy would also not be at ease. As it is, she was grappling with her illness, wondering what was wrong with her and also questioning why the whole family was all of a sudden spending all its time with her. All she knew was that she had a tumour in her brain which we'd told her would be removed and she'd be fine. But she knew there was more to it as she was in pain and was weakening.

"The doctors had said that it was only a matter of time for hers was a terminal disease. We had two options before us. One was to put all else on hold and wait. But wait for what? For her to pass on? That would have been inadvisable. So we decided to go with the other option which was to enjoy whatever time we had left with her in the right spirit and work on the Gujarat project."

Every step Ramesh Chandra took threw up a challenge more formidable than the previous one. This time too, the DB team was up against enormous odds. "Gujarat was a bigger and tougher market than any that we'd entered earlier," Sudhir pointed out. "For instance, way back in 2002, *Gujarat Samachar* had a reserve of almost Rs 400 crore in their balance sheet. In terms of money and muscle power it was huge. It was much more than our annual turnover. But it didn't bother Papa or us. Sometimes ignorance is bliss. Because those days we didn't even understand what reserve was, we shrugged it off as the other party having a lot of money. We were blissful that we had what we needed."

Ramesh Chandra's casino-swagger and relish for taking risks came into focus again. Like he had ploughed all his profits from Madhya Pradesh into Rajasthan, *Bhaskar*'s annual profit of Rs 50 to 60 crore went into their first year of business in Gujarat.

The basic moves of Ramesh Chandra's new, calculated gamble remained unchanged—prime land, a magnificent structure and an intensive, extensive market survey.

"Gujarat was a large, two-player market with a big gap between its No. 1 (*Gujarat Samachar*) and No. 2 (*Sandesh*) newspapers which firmed our decision to venture into the state, starting with an edition in Ahmedabad. We had to go in for a much larger survey in Gujarat because of the huge population in Ahmedabad. With a 1000-strong force on the ground, we interviewed nearly 10 lakh households in and around the city, as against the 2 lakh we had done in Rajasthan. So the scale and size of our Gujarat survey was almost five times that of what we had done earlier. But by then our team was also more organised and more experienced, and we had the lessons learnt from earlier experiences to guide us."

But this time, they were dealing with a readership that spoke a different language and followed a different culture.

"Even their outlook was different," noted Sudhir. "Gujaratis don't splurge money on food and clothes. In Rajasthan, they'd lay out a spread of 20 dishes for a guest whereas Gujaratis would be more balanced. In Rajasthan, women didn't have a say. In Gujarat, women were equal readers and equal players. So it was a new challenge and that's what made it more of a thrill for us."

For all the expertise they'd gained over the years, Ramesh Chandra, his sons and his core team had to go back to being students—they had to take lessons in Gujarati. As per practice, the Agarwal *parivaar* also moved to Gujarat and set up temporary residence with Sudhir's daughter even going to school in Ahmedabad.

The main thrust was to think like a homegrown Gujarati and erase the thought that they were outsiders. It had to begin with the right name.

"The moment you call yourself *Dainik Bhaskar Gujarati*, people would think you were a Hindi newspaper translated into Gujarati. We didn't want that," Sudhir disclosed. "We gave it much thought. There was no such word as '*dainik*' in Gujarati; the word for 'daily' was not '*dainik*' in Gujarati. Finally, we decided to call it *Divya Bhaskar* which was new and different. Christening our paper *Divya Bhaskar* was a big move."

Ramesh Chandra's tried-and-tested concept of going to the people and asking them what they wished for in a newspaper and following it up with the announcement, 'Now your wish will prevail' or '*Havey chalse tamhari marzi*' as a Gujarati would say it, worked like magic. It was a refreshing change especially because a top-down approach had existed so far in the state where the leading newspapers were designed by editors and readers had no say in it.

"In fact, Gujarat was an extreme case where the newspapers were considered very difficult to handle in every which way," remarked Sudhir. "When we went to invite top politicians to our launch, they too talked of the owners of both the top papers as ruthless people whose word was law. We had handled one in Rajasthan, here there were two and they were far more difficult to deal with. They were also massive size-wise."

If the fight was tougher, the victory was that much more exhilarating.

"When we launched on 22 June 2003, Chief Minister Narendra Modi said in his inaugural speech, 'A Gujarati won't buy even a cup of *chai* without taking a sip, without getting a taste of it. And you have booked 4.5 lakh copies without even showing us the paper. That's really praiseworthy.' Gujaratis are conscious of money, time, effort and delivery."

Going into Gujarat in December 2002 and launching within 189 days was another triumphant episode for the joint family that stayed together, moved together and operated together, especially considering it was a private, painful period for Ramesh Chandra and his children. For, it was while they were in the throes of opening their Gujarat chapter that Sharda Devi began to have memory lapses. She would mix up her daughters-in-law's names, forget why she'd gone into a room to talk to someone and feel drained out. She was not even 55 years old but when life was going as scripted, it didn't strike anybody to take her memory losses seriously for they often joked with her, 'Mummy, you're getting old.' The family was completely unprepared for calamitous times when the partner who had spurred Ramesh Chandra on from one adventure to another and had given him the wind beneath his wings, was handed a dire medical diagnosis. The sons and their wives closed ranks and decided not to tell Ramesh Chandra the whole truth; so he only knew that she was ailing and had no other details about her condition. The close-knit family kept its chin up and went about the Gujarat launch like it was business as usual. But as the days sped by, it was actually a devastated unit that was counting the hours.

While keeping close tabs on her health, the survey and construction work went on cheek-by-jowl, the world only seeing a professional, passionate team that came with the formidable reputation of not having lost a match so far. And Ramesh Chandra's time-tested method of announcing his arrival in a city remained unchanged as, long before Bhaskar Bhavan reached its brick and mortar stage, the brief he gave his sons was that the DB building had to be a befitting reply to the general derision they were facing.

Sudhir recalled, "My father was told that Shreyansh bhai (of *Gujarat Samachar*) was such a huge entity, who are you compared to him?'"

Ramesh Chandra's answer to that was epic, as always. As Sudhir remembered wistfully, "Papa always thought of everything on such a grand, magnificent scale, I don't think we have still been able to imbibe that from him."

An interesting sidelight everywhere that DB went was the *Vaastu*-compliance of their structures and offices. Ramesh Chandra was a strong believer in *Vaastu Shastra,* the traditional Indian science of architecture that describes the principles of design, layout, measurements, ground preparation, space arrangement and spatial geometry.

According to Hemchandra Pande, an astrologer and *Vaastu* expert, Ramesh Chandra sought his advice on which direction the top executives of DB should face while sitting in their offices.

Combining all the elements, from very inspired work to *Vaastu*, led to such a high yield that, "It was a phenomenal experience," said RD Bhatnagar, who also took lessons in Gujarati along with the rest of the core team. "We worked like an army. It was a different *josh*, energy we had. We actually got used to that kind of pace."

For Ramesh Chandra, the focus was on disproving the established order's conviction that an 'outsider' wouldn't be able to read the pulse of Gujarat. He could march on regardless because of an inner belief that however different a language may be, the emotions of an Indian were universal. He was spot on as DB took off with a print run of 4,52,000 copies.

On 22 June 2003, the stage glittered as Ramesh Chandra Agarwal proudly launched *Divya Bhaskar*, the Gujarati edition of his paper in the presence of Deputy Prime Minister Lal Krishna Advani, Union Minister for Information & Broadcasting Ravi Shankar Prasad, and four leading Chief Ministers of North India, Narendra Modi (Gujarat), Ashok Gehlot (Rajasthan), Digvijaya Singh (MP) and Ajit Jogi (Chhattisgarh).

However, despite being an occasion that called for the celebration of unparalleled success, only a few who were in the know could discern the absence of festive enthusiasm on the face of the Chairman and his sons. The harsh secret they hid from public view was that Sharda Devi was fast losing her battle with the malignant disease.

Sharda Devi had stood by Ramesh Chandra through rough times and riches. Even when he'd battled Chief Minister Arjun Singh's forces many moons ago in Gwalior, she'd left three of her children in Bhopal and occupied the chair next to her husband, never once weakening in her support. She was the source of his strength. And now, her life was abating. Only a close group of family-like team players were aware of how the Agarwal family coped with the compulsions of their Ahmedabad mission when their thoughts were centred around a loved one who was battling for her life.

When Sharda Devi's condition became critical, she wished to go back home to Bhopal. Before leaving Ahmedabad, Ramesh Chandra and Sudhir told their small group of insiders that they were leaving a 15-day-old infant in their care. They placed their trust in the team's ability to take decisions in their absence, instructing it to only convene a daily meeting and send the minutes to Bhopal.

In September 2003, a readership survey by AC Nielsen ORG MARG announced that *Divya Bhaskar* was the most-read newspaper in Ahmedabad with 12.11 lakh readers. *Gujarat Samachar* was placed second with 10.02 lakh readers.

But at home, Sharda Devi's battle went on for six months until she slipped away on 2 January 2004.

Son-in-law Vishal Agarwal for whom the Gujarat launch was his first experience as an onlooker, commented, "Despite the crisis in the family, it was phenomenal to see the kind of commitment and speed at which they launched *Divya Bhaskar*."

The personal crisis notwithstanding, Ramesh Chandra didn't ease up after launching his edition in Ahmedabad.

"The story that began in Jaipur was repeated in Gujarat too as the Chairman decided that we should start editions in Rajkot, Baroda and Surat also," disclosed Sanjay Jain.

Setting up shop in Surat came with its own trove of memorable trivia. "When we were looking for land, we heard about two theatres that were on sale," Sanjay recalled. "When I went to look at them, I saw that in one of the theatres, we could fit the printing press with minimum demolition in minimum time. The measurements were precisely what we needed for the press which was the first thing that had to be installed. Offices could always be made later. Only the old-style balcony had to go. Otherwise the whole auditorium was large enough to have the printing press there.

"Once the decision was taken, after the 9 pm to midnight show, the next morning the demolition squad moved in," he laughed. "The other theatre was pulled down and we constructed an RCC four-floor building for editorial and other offices.

"In Baroda, the 189-day period was cut down to 130 during which time we built the entire press and the office on a green field. In this manner, our benchmarks became tighter and tighter," he said, his eyes lighting up at the many challenges they had met head on.

Much like his father, Sudhir too had his sights set on what seemed like an impossible destination: he wanted to be the Indian *Asaahi Shimboon*. Started in 1879 in Osaka, Japan, *Asaahi Shimboon* was among the largest-selling newspapers of the world with a daily circulation of more than 1.25 crore copies. With in-house reporters and photographers using one of their half-a-dozen company planes, they were known to fly from Japan to London to cover events like the coronation ceremony of Queen Elizabeth of Britain. Sudhir could not breach the record set by the Japanese media wonder but he did put DB in an elevated bracket as one of the Top 5 newspapers of the world.

DB notched up bumper figures in North West and Central India, making its presence felt in Punjab, Himachal Pradesh and later, Bihar and Jharkhand too.

But what made Ramesh Chandra a phenomenal success was that he was much more than a businessman. He was also creatively perspicacious.

"During our launches," Jagdish Sharma pointed out, "we often worked with big advertising agencies for them to suggest the right line for our campaign. But most of the time, it was Rameshji who'd come up with the right thought within minutes. I have never met anybody else who could find a simple way out of every complicated situation. When we were launching in Punjab, a big agency in Delhi couldn't offer us anything creatively new and advised us to go down the same route that we had taken before. It was Rameshji who hit the nail on the head and drew the attention of the agency to the general personality of a Punjabi. He said, 'Punjabis are a hot-blooded, gregarious race. You need a campaign line that will shake them up. When the Punjabi dances, it's so robust that the earth quakes. Come up with something that aggressively questions, like *Punjab ko chahiye jawab* (Punjab demands an answer).' That became our line for the campaign."

However, when Ramesh Chandra left Gujarat to be with his wife who was weakening by the day, somebody must have sincerely told him, '*Avjo*' which in Gujarati means, 'Come back soon'.

Because the Chairman was never completely convinced that they had put optimum efforts into their Gujarat sector. The gameplan that had worked in Rajasthan was implemented here too and the group quickly stretched out to other cities in the state as well. But, for the first time, the family's collective attention was divided as mentally and emotionally, all of them were in Bhopal with Sharda Devi. Even after she passed away, it took a while for all of them to get up and really get going with life. That was why, however big the Gujarat story, Ramesh Chandra always felt they hadn't done full justice, hadn't fully exploited the state's immense potential. He would one day return to it and make it his swan song.

14 years after his mother passed away, Pawan was able to talk about it objectively.

"Yeah, Gujarat couldn't get our full attention because all of us shifted back to Bhopal. In all our other projects, we had stayed on in the respective cities after the launch and done our best to watch it grow. This time, we couldn't. But Papa did take it over again towards the end of his life. And he was like a man completely recharged when he returned to Gujarat (13 years after the first launch in Ahmedabad).

"He was so happy taking charge of it again, he did things which we wouldn't have thought of. We grew by almost 15 per cent within a few months of Papa taking charge of Gujarat again."

But back in 2005, Ramesh Chandra's team thought they would all have to start saying, '*Vannakkam*' or '*Bhalo*', as they were asked to prepare themselves to conquer yet another state, another new language. They talked amongst themselves and wondered, are we going South, do we have to learn Tamil? That seemed so far-fetched that by elimination, they zeroed in on Bengal as their next stop. Besides, Sudhir had also pointed them eastwards, given them a circulation figure and asked them to make a full project report of the space, machines and manpower they would need. He told them to bring it with them to a meeting in Mumbai, complete with costs and a timeline.

It was only at this meeting that Ramesh Chandra and Sudhir revealed their hand—they were going to enter Mumbai to bring out a daily newspaper in English!

Ramesh Chandra was going to have a head-on collision with the biggest of them all in the most bustling commercial capital of the country—*The Times Of India* in Mumbai.

In January 2005, when Ramesh Chandra and Sudhir asked their inner circle to move to Mumbai and check out the lay of the land, the team moved with trademark swiftness and set up a printing press in six months' time.

"It was the toughest job we'd done so far because we wanted a unique configuration of machines, one that had never been done before anywhere in the world," Sanjay said, still energised by how they'd pulled it off.

Girish who had temporarily shifted to Mumbai to set up the national ad sales of the DB group in 2004, was the man on the ground. Privy to every heartbeat and heartbreak of their new paper, Girish filed Ramesh Chandra's intensely fought *DNA* story.

"After Gujarat," he said, "somebody had told Sudhirbhai that it was time for us to look at the national stage, that we should be in Mumbai." The year 2004 was when cities and metros like Delhi and Mumbai were the premium markets and looked at as different from the rest of India. They were the upper crust where real, big-time money was being generated.

Ramesh Chandra had been tossing around in his head the idea of a newspaper in English for quite a while. So, when Sudhir echoed the thought, Ramesh Chandra looked at the 'bigger market, bigger money' opportunity and said, 'Let's do it'.

At the turn of the century, an English newspaper in Mumbai was the ultimate sign that a newspaper had arrived on the national scene. But it was going to be an enterprise of such un-factored magnitude that Ramesh Chandra halted to ponder if he needed to reinforce himself with additional firepower. For the first time, he decided to go into partnership—with Subhash Chandra, the head honcho of Zee TV. It was, amusingly, the coming together of two men who were not truly proficient in English.

On their father's instructions, when his sons went to talk to Subhash Chandra, the media man didn't hesitate even for a minute.

"Subhashji was just like my dad, he took instant decisions and said, 'Yes, let's do it' on the spot," noted Girish. "That's how *DNA* was started."

"*DNA* came about because there was mutual trust and faith in each other," explained the Chairman of Essel Group, Subhash Chandra. "Rameshji came to me and shared his thoughts on starting an English newspaper in Mumbai. He told me why he wanted to start it, even though *The Times Of India* already had a monopoly here. But the advertising revenue was so high in Mumbai etc. He said he wanted to do it with me, *saath mein karenge* (we'll do it together). I told him, let's go ahead, I'm willing to invest capital in it but I have no experience in this field, so you will have to run it. We shook hands and it started."

They were already friends, so he must've known enough about DB's stout financial health before taking the decision.

"I was aware and also not aware of their growth story," he answered. "Where there's friendship, you don't quite go looking at their balance sheet. But yes, I was aware of how they'd gone to Gujarat and Rajasthan. I was there when they launched Gujarat, I was with them in Rajasthan also. I had witnessed it all first-hand."

"Psychologically, Mumbai was a bigger market for us," Girish analysed how the *DNA* experience was in a league bigger than any they'd ever known. "In a metro, in English, and we were essentially desi folks. It was also completely different working with a partner for the first time. Not being answerable to anybody and being conscious that your partner should never feel he's not been consulted or been a part of decision making, were two different worlds. Although one must emphasise that Subhashji never interfered, we were wired in such a way that we didn't want a situation where it could be said that this was what I wanted but you didn't pay heed to it."

In a city like Mumbai where real estate prices forced even the wealthy to pause before spending, the hunt was only for appropriate property for the printing press which was found in Navi Mumbai. The logistics and the mental makeup of the city with high-rises were so completely different from any place they'd known so far that there was no grandiose plan for a building to make a statement.

Instead, Girish channelised his energies into building the brand, especially after a friend goaded him into action.

"A friend said to me, 'Mumbai is different, you won't be able to create a brand pre-launch.' I thought to myself that if we put up 40-50 hoardings in Gujarat and Rajasthan, we'd go for 200 hoardings in Mumbai. But we actually ended up putting some 500 hoardings all over Mumbai. I said, we'll capture the market."

But like it was in Gujarat, they had to first christen the

baby before introducing it to the world. Pradeep Guha, former president of The Times of India Group, whose name was suggested by Subhash Chandra, was the de facto CEO of the new company which Ramesh Chandra and Subhash Chandra had started to facilitate their new paper. Girish and Pradeep, along with Rediff, the ad agency they had hired, brainstormed over the right name. Predictable titles like 'The Daily Sun' (a literal translation of *Dainik Bhaskar*), 'The Sun' and 'The Morning Star' were briefly discussed and quickly discarded. Girish hit upon the idea of going for an abbreviation, an acronym like ASAP, and the creative director of Rediff came up with *DNA*.

Girish's first reaction was that it sounded like a medical journal. But when the agency head explained to him that *DNA* was the short form of Daily News Analysis, it was discussed with Ramesh Chandra and Subhash Chandra. "Everybody felt it was a unique name which was what we were looking for. So *DNA* it was," Girish explained.

This time, Ramesh Chandra didn't go for the jugular of the main newspaper in town. He aimed for the respectable position of the No. 2 newspaper in Mumbai. Girish endorsed it: "We always had the No. 2 position as our target."

The survey teams were togged up in smart outfits designed by Manish Malhotra. But Mumbai had a lifestyle vastly different from the rest of India. This was a city where nobody had the luxury of time. Too busy to read in the morning and too exhausted at the end of the day to welcome an unknown visitor, most offices and residences were also manned by security guards. Going up and knocking on anybody's door was not an accepted part of the culture. To further confound and stonewall the DB team, it was a multi-lingual city with Marathi, English, Gujarati and then Hindi being spoken in that order of preference.

"The complications were many. In Mumbai, one needed permission from the housing society to knock on the doors of its residents. We faced a problem in posh localities," accepted Girish. "But our large team engaged with about 10 lakh people in our 3-month door-to-door contact programme where we pre-booked 3.5 lakh copies."

As per *Bhaskar* routine, ideas, opinions and suggestions collated from the surveys were put under the scanner. It threw up the important point that *TOI* was perceived as a newspaper of the rich and the elite. *DNA* decided to reach out to anybody who could read English.

It was a territory with its own peculiarities. "In this city, you needed to tell people a lot about yourself, blow your own trumpet, and announce that you can do it. You had to make a lot more noise," remarked Girish. "The other side of it was that we got more notice in Mumbai than in Gujarat or Rajasthan where we'd done an equally major or an even bigger job. In Mumbai, people were noticing you, talking about you, monitoring you. There were articles on us in the media."

Girish took a call that he himself would step away from the spotlight with only Ramesh Chandra as the face of DB. "It was DB and Zee. I was the operating director but I decided that I shouldn't be seen. Subhashji had no objections, it was all my own sense of ethics and what I felt was the right thing to do."

But they couldn't control the external forces.

Ramesh Chandra was not alone in wanting the No. 2 position in Mumbai. *Hindustan Times* had decided to enter the same territory and was eyeing the same slot.

With *DNA* and *Hindustan Times* poised to attack his fortress, Sameer Jain of Bennett Coleman sat up alert. *HT* was a known opponent as they had been locking horns in Delhi for years. But Jain hadn't crossed swords with *Bhaskar* so far although Ramesh Chandra Agarwal's reputation preceded him. The media world was only too aware of his historic forays into territories where he had tired out and defeated unchallenged stalwarts like *Nai*

Duniya, Navbharat, Rajasthan Patrika, The Tribune, Punjab Kesri and *Gujarat Samachar*. So Sameer Jain fortified his garrison.

The Times Of India or the Old Lady of Bori Bunder (as the paper was called) also had a trick or two up her sleeve to disarm those who were setting foot in her territory. *TOI*'s Sameer Jain picked up where *DNA* had its eye—on the No. 2 position in Mumbai. *TOI* saw no reason why it couldn't snatch the position for itself and be both No. 1 and No. 2. In one of the smartest moves in the publishing world, *TOI* launched its own tabloid *Mumbai Mirror* in double quick time which soon staked its claim as the 1st runner-up to the parent newspaper.

"While we were getting ready to launch *DNA, Hindustan Times* also came to Mumbai. So we had an additional contender in the fray," Girish reiterated. "And *TOI* launched *Mumbai Mirror.* But we didn't look at that too much because it was a tabloid while we were launching a broad sheeter."

The *DB* team was too dynamised to harbour any hesitancy. The news that *HT* was also entering the arena didn't dilute Sudhir's conviction. Instead, it began to look even more enticing—Mumbai was the boom city where advertisement revenues and business thrived like no other part of India. *TOI* had struck gold here and mined it for 170 years. The Mumbai edition of *TOI* mopped up more ad revenue for its owners, Bennett Coleman & Co than the combined collections of all their other editions.

TOI struck in all directions. *TOI* also started block booking ads with deals struck and locked for three years.

"That was a move I hadn't anticipated," admitted Girish who was caught off guard by the sucker punch. "*TOI* was the biggest and they tied up with advertisers for exclusivity. The understanding was, give ads only to *TOI*, not to *DNA* or *HT*, and I'll give you this massive discount. It was an 'I'm willing to bleed but I'll stop you guys' move. It hit us because we lost out on revenue. We hadn't foreseen it because it was unheard of that you decide to bleed to such an extent."

Caught off-guard but confident about building his brand, Girish continued to bombard the city with hoardings. He launched the compelling campaign, 'Speak up, it's in your DNA' with the visual of young people with their lips sealed with tape. For the first time, the busy Mumbaikar stopped, looked and realised that somebody very creative and compelling was coming to the city.

"I was once having lunch with Mr Ratan Tata and he said to me, 'That was the biggest and most impactful campaign I've ever seen,'" disclosed Girish. "Coming from Mr Tata, it was high praise indeed. Thus, we had created the brand before the launch."

It certainly succeeded in rattling an established behemoth which couldn't afford to be complacent.

It was the toughest fight that *TOI* ever had as Subhash Chandra and Ramesh Chandra (not related by blood but belonging to the same Vaish community and sharing a common birthday on 30 November) were both battle-hardened veterans in their respective fields. When he set up Zee TV, Subhash Chandra had taken on ferocious global media maharaja Rupert Murdoch and not buckled once as he established a mighty empire of his own. Ramesh Chandra's exploits in the newspaper world were so well-chronicled that he relished the reputation of being a giant slayer.

But *DNA* was also Ramesh Chandra's hardest battle where it seemed like hurdles were springing up all around.

With unprecedented incidents like a machine getting so heated up in the printing press that its components melted and an accident where a staffer nearly lost a limb, it was literally blood and sweat that went into the production of *DNA*.

At one stage, sensing the despair of the crew, Sudhir sent them his favourite poem, '*Koshish karnewalon ki...*'—an inspirational poem that lifted spirits and exhorted the staff to keep doing their best. For, success came only to the truly industrious.

But to top their woes, nature unleashed its fury on the city five days before *DNA* was to be launched. Following a cloudburst, an unprecedented, incessant downpour and extreme high tides submerged Mumbai.

"The amount of rain was unbelievable," RD recalled. "The entire family, all the three brothers, their wives and Chairman Sir were all at the plant. We also took spiritual help—there were pundits performing puja with the family, everybody praying that nothing should go wrong. But it rained cats and dogs relentlessly and amidst all this, we got the information that two of our colleagues were in danger of getting drowned. Their car had already sunk beneath water, but we managed to get a crane, lower its hook, break the windshield and pull them out in time. Along with them, a third man who we didn't even know, also got pulled out. His car had drowned earlier. By God's grace, all of them were saved."

Girish described the circumstances around which they launched DNA on 30 July 2005.

"Suddenly, just a few days before our launch on 30 July, it started pouring. On 26 July, Mumbai was marooned. People weren't able to reach their homes. We got quilts and mattresses for our staff who were stranded in the office to sleep on. My house was close by in Worli, so food was prepared for everybody and sent to the office. Till the 28th, there was no let-up in the downpour and we wondered if we should postpone our launch. But we took a call on it and decided to stick to our date. It was a daily newspaper, not a monthly, and conditions would improve by the day. So we launched DNA on 30 July as scheduled. Some people felt it wasn't a great product. But only we knew how tough it had been to bring it out with 50 per cent of the staff unable to even reach office. Without the edit and technical staff or the secretaries or page-makers, and the many hurdles it faced, the skeleton team managed to do a great job. It was an unbelievable experience."

But this time, the story came with a dampener.

"We started with 3.5 lakh copies. But the numbers stagnated at that mark and didn't move up," Girish stated frankly. "This was unlike the other markets where we had witnessed a healthy spurt in growth. In Mumbai, *HT* was also hitting a 2.5 lakh circulation. With two big new players coming in, there wasn't the kind of growth we'd seen elsewhere. Count *Mumbai Mirror* too and the market was saturated. *TOI* was doing about 6 lakh copies. Practically overnight, the market doubled.

"We created a great product, got great editorial reviews and a decent circulation. But unfortunately, DNA couldn't live up to our expectations in terms of growth, revenue, or circulation," he observed.

"In 2007, we changed the whole working—got a new CEO and a new editorial team. Things improved for a while but in 2008-09, the Lehmann Brothers episode happened and by the time the country came out of that market freefall, we found that a paradigm shift had taken place. The big metros had got saturated and the advertising and marketing money was shifting to Tier 2 and Tier 3 cities. That's when terms such as Tier 2 and Tier 3 began to be heard more frequently. When we reviewed the situation with Papa, we realised that the English newspaper market was no longer growing. So we had to deliberate on whether we really wanted to commit that capital to a market where we saw no future growth."

The biggest achievement was that *DNA* got the *TOI* bosses worried enough to move out of their ivory tower in Delhi and come down to the battleground. Which wasn't much of a solace when Ramesh Chandra saw his balance sheet bleeding.

Faced with a huge investment that was impossible to recover and too many other forces working against them, Ramesh Chandra and Sudhir had to take a business decision that was a wrench, one of the toughest they'd taken in their lives. In 2011, they stepped out of *DNA* and their victorious juggernaut halted.

"With a heavy heart, and for the first time in any state, we decided to pull out of DNA," Girish said. "Papa was quite okay with the idea and Subhashji was gracious enough to say, 'I'm fine with your decision, I'll run it, you can move on'. Both of us had lost a substantial amount of money on it by then."

"The end of the partnership made no difference to our friendship. Not even 1 per cent," averred Subhash Chandra who continued to back the paper. "Many mistakes happen. Mistakes were made but you don't blame anybody for it. I don't think they're relevant today. It was my choice to stay with *DNA*, I could've closed it down.

"Their financial circumstances must've been such that they wanted to withdraw from it. We had no fight or anything of the sort over it.

"There was quite a huge loss," he admitted. "I won't disclose what it was but Rameshji told me that they had incurred losses elsewhere, and circumstances were not allowing them to continue. He and Sudhirbhai explained their circumstances to me, they were straightforward about it."

So far, one had seen Ramesh Chandra grow tall as a conqueror. But what was a rare human story, was that he grew even taller in defeat.

"I really admired my father at this juncture because pulling out was a decision taken by Papa and Sudhirbhai, and they did it with cool-headed maturity," observed Girish. "They said, 'Let's cut our losses and move on. Why put good money into something bad?' All Papa said was, 'Let's learn from whatever mistakes we made and improve our act.' I loved his attitude."

It wasn't only about the heaps of money lost. It was also about facing public defeat like a man.

"To be honest, it was not only a huge amount of money lost, it was a loss to reputation also," accepted Girish. "But it was more in the minds of others than in our own. Fortunately,

Bhaskar itself was big enough with its growth story so clearly on the ascendant that it helped cushion the jolt. We launched in Punjab in 2007, in Jharkhand in 2010 and in Maharashtra in 2012. So we kept expanding and growing, went public too with an IPO in 2010, and became a billion-dollar listed company. So there were enough good things happening to balance out the *DNA* fiasco. But yes, there were great learnings from Mumbai. It was essentially about how to deal with a joint venture and a big new market."

Ramesh Chandra snapped out of the setback and steamed ahead, never once wincing that he hadn't won the English market.

"In his mind, it wasn't the language," Girish corrected the perception. "It was about wanting to operate from Delhi and Mumbai to break into the national market. It was about the national market and not about English, he was not obsessed with it. Far from it. When we were doing *DNA*, it's not as if he strutted around and thought he had arrived. When we pulled out too, he simply asked us to shut it down. It was a calculated business call. I loved that about him and I still need to learn that from him."

The staff and core team that had shed blood to repeat the triumphs of the past couldn't take this defeat with the same equanimity as their Chairman.

"Despite all the money and effort, it's true that *DNA* did not give us the success we expected," Sanjay Jain said sadly. But he strongly felt that *DB* would've pulled it off if it had gone into battle on its own.

However devastated the team was, RD marvelled at how Ramesh Chandra didn't even twitch a muscle.

"I never saw his facial expression change even in a calamitous situation such as this one," remarked RD. "He was still very optimistic. Even after *DNA*, he was so undeterred, did so many other launches. He launched Maharashtra, he launched Bihar. We can't touch the kind of positivity and calmness he possessed."

It was like the stonecutter who kept hammering away at a big boulder. The rock didn't flinch but the stone cutter kept at it, days turned into weeks, weeks into months. Until one day, the rock cracked open. But he knew that it wasn't the last round of hammering that did it. It was the collective power of all those months of labour that made the rock finally give up and render the stonecutter's efforts fruitful. Similarly, Ramesh Chandra wanted the big rock to split open and he hammered away cheerfully, knowing that one day *DB* would be No. 1.

If the scintillating launch of *Divya Bhaskar* was dimmed by a very heavy personal loss, the *DNA* story was clouded by an exceptional professional setback.

'There is defeat for everyone at some time in their lives. Some are destroyed by defeat, and some made small and mean by victory. Greatness lives in one who triumphs equally over defeat and victory'. Nobel Prize winner John Steinbeck's lines were a wrap-up of Ramesh Chandra's persona. He was neither destroyed by defeat nor rendered mean by victory and he emerged magnanimous, triumphing equally over defeat and victory.

For Ramesh Chandra, every reversal was like the hammer on the rock. It explained his equanimity even after taking the tough call on *DNA*. With his mind eternally seeking new thought and new avenues, he made confident forays into real estate, malls, hotels and the power sector.

While launches galore went on in the newspaper world, an important addition was made to the *DB* family in another sector.

Amongst bureaucrats of all cadres and levels and in political circles that leaned right or left, one of Ramesh Chandra's *coup de maître* that all of them knew about was the rabbit he pulled out of a magic hat, and placed as his man in Delhi. The induction of a man of medicine into the hurly-burly of business and politics came from Ramesh Chandra's bag of unexpected tricks.

Dr Bharat Agarwal was a medical student in Indore where he and Sudhir (who was then managing the DB edition there) became friends. But it was when Bharat moved to Mumbai to do his post-graduation at Jaslok Hospital that he met the man who would one day turn out to be his mentor, father figure and closest companion. For Ramesh Chandra, it was like chancing upon a fourth son in whom he could repose complete trust about company matters, who became his trusted lieutenant and indispensable liaison man in Delhi.

In 1992, Ramesh Chandra was flying into Mumbai with his wife and Girish; Sudhir had phoned Bharat to meet them at the airport. They had an appointment at Tata Memorial Hospital for Sharda Devi and had come prepared for a prolonged stay if her treatment demanded it. But luckily, it was a false alarm, as a mammograph cleared all their doubts and the relieved Agarwal family could jubilantly head back home to celebrate Holi.

However, that meeting brought together a medical student and a hard-nosed businessman, a duo that had only a surname in common.

Ramesh Chandra cannily sized-up the man as more suitable for power and politics than for stethoscopes and surgeries. To expect the doctor to jump ship and settle down with such cosy ease in the political corridors of Delhi required a scout who could sense the restless potential in him. But Ramesh Chandra was also sharp enough to see that this was not a newspaper man, he had assets that would be of use in Delhi. So, to begin with, Dr Bharat Agarwal was made CEO of a company far removed from DB. Ramesh Chandra had formed a new FMCG division named Bhaskar Global which sold only one product—Bhaskar Salt. The freshly appointed CEO thus began with selling salt.

The salt business didn't last. Bharat Agarwal did.

But selling salt had never been of any particular interest to Ramesh Chandra. Bharat revealed that what had brought salt and a medicine man into the Chairman's line of vision was a study of the stars above—astrology.

"Rameshji strongly believed in astrology. It was suggested to him that if he dabbled in this business, it would give him good dividends. So the first FMCG was white salt." Bharat's horoscope was also found compatible for FMCG.

From selling salt in Bhopal to politicking in Delhi was a major jump. "One fine evening in 2003, I was made executive director of the group," said Bharat. "Rameshji told me, 'I'm shifting you to Delhi and the sole purpose is for you to represent a social, political and bureaucratic connect.'"

What Bharat admired was Ramesh Chandra's insatiable thirst to keep acquiring knowledge. "I think that fire to learn stayed with him till the day he collapsed. We'd gone to China a couple of years before he passed away and he was curious about everything. He met manufacturers, went to an industrial zone, went to offices, he just wanted to know what was happening there, what made China grow. He was so inquisitive. His father gave him just an edition. He diversified into solvent, textiles, real estate, different kinds of trading. He did gold trading too at one time when there was a gold scheme. He was so passionate, he was learning every day of his life."

Even if Ramesh Chandra pulled out of a couple of businesses after venturing into them, his passion never wilted. He went into every new venture with the enthusiasm of a neophyte. He never did anything casually, indifferently.

Being a people's person, he also revelled in leading a team. Bharat described Ramesh Chandra's modus operandi by which he cajoled a prize performance out of those around him.

"He wanted everything to be done as of yesterday," he noted, "and with the way he motivated people, it did get done yesterday. He wouldn't just talk to people, he would give them the way forward too. He would guide them, do the hand-holding and make sure the work was done."

"The important point was," said Bharat, "he connected with everybody, from the Prime Minister to the common man. His behaviour, his language, his communication would not vary. He firmly believed that one needed a variety of life around oneself. One of his famous lines was, '*Yeh jivan Shivji ki baraat hai*'. Life is like Lord Shiva's wedding procession which must have elephants, horses, snakes, and all sorts of life featured in it. That's why he always expounded that you cannot live with only one set of people. We need all kinds around us, each set having some relevance and importance in your progress through life."

However, *Bhaskar* remained his first love. Even when he took his last breath, Ramesh Chandra had his boots on more as a newspaperman than a businessman. It was the world of news dissemination that gave him recognition nonpareil and gave him his biggest joys as he transformed that small, nondescript daily from Bhopal into a flourishing empire.

A heap of awards came his way during his lifetime. These included the National Citizen Award (2001) for journalism, Samaj Seva Samman, the Ernst & Young Entrepreneur Award for which he was a finalist, and Acharya Tulsi Samman.

The Rajiv Gandhi Lifetime Achievement Award that was conferred on him, his inclusion in three annual editions of *India Today* which put him on the list of the 50 most powerful people in the country, and *Forbes* placing him at the 95th position in the list of India's richest people, were all resounding applause for the newspaperman.

Under him, DB kept taking jumbo strides in journalism.

His entrepreneurial nature which got enhanced because of his inborn curiosity, led to Ramesh Chandra willing to try anything new that was on offer. When the I&B Ministry opened up its second phase of FM radio stations to private parties, his company was right there to put in its tender. His trusted foot soldiers, who were always on the go and as gung-ho as him to explore the untested, were happy that they could execute launches that went beyond a new edition of the printed newspaper.

DB won all the 17 stations it bid for with the clear strategy of establishing Hindi FM channels in the areas which were its core strength. There was thus a synergy since the radio stations were launched in places where Ramesh Chandra already had his newspaper.

Editorially, there was never a pause in the creativity.

That it was never about pure business alone for Ramesh Chandra but was also about using the medium for societal betterment, was tangible with the emphasis given to NNN—No Negative News.

With the world living off stark, cold and heartbreaking stories of war and sorrow in practically every area of human life, *Bhaskar* introduced a unique No Negative News (NNN) concept in its paper every Monday. The positivity and novelty of this was noted by Prime Minister Narendra Modi who greatly appreciated it in a speech he made in Canada. The NNN tradition has continued in DB.

At every turn, Ramesh Chandra's personal philosophy was reflected and there was a twin thrust—boost readership but also nurture social issues. For even as he kept establishing and reinforcing the DB brand, he continued looking at profit as a by-product, never as the sole motivator of his life.

"Way back in 1986-87, both my parents showed a marked inclination to help others," remarked Girish.

"It started as a small counselling session for people. I used to watch with wonder as my parents would mediate in the marital and family issues of relatives and family friends.

"They were also involved with the Agarwal *samaj*, our community. They actively participated in marriage and matchmaking programmes and I would get very upset with that," he confessed. "I wondered why they were wasting their time on other people's problems, why people had to come to our house to unburden themselves with their sob stories. Papa never tried to explain himself to us. He did what he wanted to do. But as I grew up, I discovered that what he did was some really fantastic work for society.

"One was a matchmaking programme. I realised its importance later in life. In middle-class and lower middle-class families, especially those days, a boy coming to see a girl was a huge event. It was expensive too for the girl's family. They'd whitewash their house and prepare an array of food items to serve. The whole community would get to know about it and the girl would be under great stress. She could be selected or rejected and the fear of the latter was palpable. She would be sized-up and there'd be much talk about it. If it fell through, there would be a buzz that these many boys had seen and rejected her, fanning the gossip that something was wrong with her and so on.

"Papa pondered over how to circumvent this. And he came up with *Parichay Sammelan,* a platform for introducing eligible girls and boys to each other. Those interested would register themselves with this *Sammelan*. Every girl and boy was given a chance to go up on stage for a minute and talk about themselves and their expections. So the families in attendance got to see all the boys and all the girls. A small area was designated where they could also meet and talk in person. With this, the trauma experienced by a girl was eliminated because she was there with 200 other girls. Whether she got rejected or selected did not become the news of the day. When Papa started the *Sammelan,* it was the need of the day.

"He also started the *samoohik vivah* or community weddings, where several couples got married at the same time. Marriage was a drain on many families. They had to host the *baraatis* (groom's party), look after their food, their stay, and there could be dowry demands too. Papa would say, society must come forward and conduct these marriages. 100 couples would get married under one roof, each couple had to pay only Rs 5,000 and the community would make all the arrangements. People would also gift fans, tables, chairs and other items which took care of a part of the dowry.

"Papa took it a step further. There was a girl who had a limp because of which she was not finding a match. Seeing this Papa announced that he was adopting this girl. Suddenly, she had many boys lined up to choose from, and she chose one guy. We took care of her wedding like we would for any family member, and to this day, she comes to our house every *Rakshabandhan* and ties a *rakhi* to all of us. She knows we're there for her even after Papa is no more. Psychologically, she knows she's got this family standing behind her."

The importance of what Ramesh Chandra did and the wisdom behind his decisions dawned on youngsters like Girish only years later.

"I used to wonder," admitted Girish, "why take a girl under your umbrella? Just pay her family some money. Dad told me later on, 'I could've announced I'm giving Rs 5 lakh for her wedding expenses. But would that have changed society? You can make a difference only when you lead by example.' Once Papa did that, others too came forward to take care of many such girls and boys."

Water conservation was another of Ramesh Chandra's social concerns. "Papa also got involved with a *pani bachao*, a 'save water' campaign. He realised that water was getting to be a problem during the summer months. So, he started a dry Holi initiative, which became a major movement. In our family too, we have been observing dry Holi for over 10 years and continue to do so. The newspaper is also involved in spreading the word."

His philanthropic bent of mind found Ramesh Chandra stepping in to help any group of people who faced a problem. "Whether it was connected with the police or any other authority, he would help them out not only through the newspaper but by also getting personally involved. He would fix a meeting with the concerned authority and send the people across to have their problems looked into.

"When I once questioned him on why he was involved with people he didn't really know, he said that people looked up to a certain person because he could help them in a situation. Getting them a hearing from a minister or anybody else in power, would benefit them. He added, 'I only recommend genuine cases. If God has given you the position, why not use it for society? If it's win-win for the government and the association, why not help facilitate it?'"

Like his business interests which were varied, his social work too took many hues.

He paid close attention even to cremation grounds. "People go there for a ritual and formality," commented Girish. "But nobody does anything to make them nicer, neater places. Papa voiced it and along with Sudhirbhai, they worked out a programme to make crematoriums look much more pleasant than they looked earlier. Everybody has to go there one day. Papa motivated us to work on it.

"I also liked the fact that it wasn't only about the Agarwal community," he added. "He was involved with the Christian community, with Muslims, the Jain *samaj*, with everybody. When Mother Theresa visited Bhopal in 1983-84, Papa helped with all the arrangements, he was right at the forefront. I was very young and though I did meet her, I didn't know much about her other than what everybody already knew, that she did some social work. Later, I realised who she was and it fascinated me that Papa was so involved with all the different communities spread across various states.

"A friend once told me that if he had any work to be done, he would not talk to me about it because I would avoid or put it off and 99 per cent of the time, I wouldn't get it done. But, he said, he would go to my father. 'I will call up your father because I know that Uncle will do his best. If he's in the office, I can just barge in and meet him. If he's busy, he'll ask me to see him at home at night or to come again the next day but he won't refuse to meet me. He'll meet me and 99 per cent of the time, he'll make every effort to get the work done.'

"I was surprised that although he was my friend, he went to my father when he needed help. But that was Papa. His office had an open-door policy. Anybody could walk in. He had no security and he had no problems with meeting anybody. He stayed connected with everybody. He was really keen to give back to society whatever he could whether it was through his *pani bachao* campaign or taking a stand against child marriage."

Ramesh Chandra also gave holistic life and spiritualism a place of importance, weaving them into his work and family spheres. In fact, rather interestingly, spiritual management guru Pt Vijayshankar Mehta drew a parallel between the success of *Bhaskar* and the *Sunderkand* of *Ramcharitmanas.* He pointed out Lord Hanuman's golden rules of never pausing to relax until it was mission accomplished, of thinking on his feet during a crisis, and of noble-mindedness and celebration when the job was done with aplomb. The learned Pandit concluded that Ramesh Chandra's success story could be traced to his effortless implementation of the management formula hidden in the *Sundarkand*.

Pawan Agarwal put into a nutshell his father's matchless vision and what gave him the power to propel DB to vertiginous heights.

"We worked like a cricket team with Papa as the Virat Kohli of our team," he said jauntily. "We always knew that he stood behind us. If one of us made a few runs less, he was there to hit the sixes. At work, he never treated us as sons, we were always colleagues. When we were in the workplace, he never ever gave us the impression that he knew more than us and he always inculcated in us the discipline of listening to each other."

Work and home operated on different planes.

"In the family we follow a hierarchy but when it came to the business, we were equals, respecting each other's opinions."

"It was Papa who would encourage us to move on from state to state. He would say, '*Chalo*, this state is set, leave it to the professionals, move to the next, forget about this one, don't keep looking back.' He would also keep telling us that there's only so much you can do in one place, learn from there and give to the next. That's how we kept working on ourselves and improving with every new launch. In the last 30 years or so, the majority of our time was spent on expanding our media network. And, of course, in the last seven years in building the power business."

A marked feature in Ramesh Chandra's personality was that he was like a lion leading his pride. He liked people. Pawan agreed, "He had only two things to say about this: either join people or get people to join you. He never worked as a loner. Whichever town he would land in, there would be hordes of people waiting to meet him. People knew that he would always have a solution to their problems."

Etched in Pawan's memory was an incident that happened a few years ago when they were working on a project that had to do with the distribution of power—essentially, electricity distribution. His father had gathered whatever information he could from engineers but still felt a certain dissatisfaction. He felt there was something that he hadn't quite grasped.

"While driving," recalled Pawan, "he saw a guy climbing an electricity pole, someone from the power department. He stopped the car, called the man over and asked him, '*Yaar*, tell me, how is electricity stolen?' He had been intrigued by the methods employed to pilfer electricity and had to understand them to be able to think of ways to prevent theft. What the engineers had told him and what the man on the ground knew was different. While the engineer knew it in bits and pieces, this man had first-hand knowledge of how it was done."

That was Ramesh Chandra's style of functioning—to understand by listening to everybody. That's where his natural humility also kicked in. He could climb down and talk to anybody.

Another substantial feature was his speed in decision-making and getting the work done, a quality much discussed by his core team too.

"He worked at lightning speed," admired Pawan. "He would think of something, and then establish an urgency to show why it needed to be done now and not one month later. He would find ways to get it done immediately or let you find it. But he would also show you what the cost would be if it was not done right now. When you saw the cost and the payoff, you would yourself get going and say, 'Get it done now'. In this way, he expanded people's minds, filled them with self-belief."

People was the keyword. He invested in people.

"He always put people at the centre of the problem and said, there is no problem which does not have a solution," said Pawan. "If you are determined, the solution will come walking to you."

Pawan gave an example of how deeply his father studied a subject before taking a call on his next move.

"At one time, he was interested in understanding the distribution of films. During an interaction with actor Aamir Khan at an event, we asked him over dinner, 'Why are films not growing in business in India? Why is it that films don't cross the Rs 200 crore mark in the North, even though they are spread over so many states, while films in a South Indian language go on to do a business of Rs 400 crore in spite of being restricted to one linguistic state?'

"Aamir told us that we had fewer screens and if we increased their number, perhaps we'd do Rs 500 crore business too. The conversation ended there. But not for Papa. Three days later, he called a distributor, a cinema owner and a producer to his office. Each of them had a different narrative, so he wanted to call all of them together and hear them out. He later concluded that it was a question of hardware, of cinemas, and not of software, of supply of films. He looked at all aspects of it, from the real estate point of view where the cinema had to be in a prime location and not on the outskirts, the Return On Investment (ROI), everything. And then he decided not to invest in it."

In that never-ending quest for expansion, it was Ramesh Chandra who decided that it was time for the family business to go public.

His belief that to really grow one needed a stronger currency than cash led him to the decision that DB had to turn into a public limited company. In 2006, Warburg Pincus, a blue chip American private equity firm, which was the only investor in Airtel at that time, came in and took a 7 per cent stake in DB with the clear understanding that this was the route to the ultimate destination of an IPO.

Pulak Chandan Prasad of Warburg, who met Ramesh Chandra purely as a businessman in 2005, had met enough people in his career as a professional to instinctively know when someone stood out as unique. DB was still a private company when they met and the plan was to professionalise the group over time, exit the private equity and go in for an IPO.

Pulak wondered why they should professionalise DB and why Ramesh Chandra would want to withdraw from it. They should be No. 1 in the business and go public a few years later.

After a three-and-a-half hour long conversation, Pulak came away impressed that Ramesh Chandra grasped what he had to say and was ready for a long-term view of what the investor would bring to the business.

By the time DB went public in 2010, Pulak had exited Warburg and set up Nalanda, his own firm. But he did invest in DB.

A few months before Ramesh Chandra passed away, when he was looking at other businesses, he had met Pulak to figure out what he could do. This was much after he had handed over his business to Sudhir, "which, incidentally, a lot of patriarchs are unable to do," commented Pulak. When it was pointed out to him that he had no in-depth insights into the other businesses that he was looking at but had enormous and phenomenal knowledge of the media world, Ramesh Chandra accepted Pulak's counsel. That's when he decided to head to Gujarat to turn DB around.

All through his life, Ramesh Chandra had his thumb rules in place with a sharpness that zeroed in on salient points. He didn't expend personal energy or time poring over mounds of research or wading through Power Point presentations and excel sheets with voluminous data. He preferred throwing questions at his team and getting his answers. He also prospered because, instead of wasting his energy resources on tiresome micro and macro operations, he stood back and looked at the vastness before him.

"Often, he would change the very paradigm of a discussion and tell us that it was not because he was smarter than everybody else but because he had walked that path before. Also, because he didn't involve himself in daily operations, he could look at the larger picture," Pawan offered a glimpse into his father's thought process. "Papa would say, 'You people are still floating in the ocean while I can provide a helicopter view of how to navigate the boat and take it to the shore.' He believed that anybody who was not in the operating seat could have a helicopter view."

Ramesh Chandra's one pet peeve was that his sons wouldn't take the big leaps of faith and the huge risks that he took all his life. He knew that commitment came with risk-taking and wished his sons would inherit that quality from him.

"You guys don't want to take a risk," he often chided them.

"All the new ventures were his ideas," Pawan put on record.

Whatever his other business interests, media was where he wanted his sons to concentrate in his lifetime.

"It was all his vision, his idea totally, where to involve us," underscored Girish. "For example, we had other businesses like textile and solvents. But he said, 'You boys concentrate on our media business.' Our textile unit in Bhopal is about 20-25 years old but I must have gone there only three times in my entire life. Because it was not my unit, my father would say, mind your business well, don't waste your time or your mental capacities on things that are not in your portfolio. My father used to manage all the other businesses with professionals."

But what he thoroughly revelled in was being a newspaper man—that gave him an unequalled high.

"He never enjoyed or used his political clout," interjected Girish. "He never enjoyed hobnobbing with politicians either. He was on his own trip."

An incredible trip that began modestly in Ibrahimpura, Bhopal, and spread to 12 states with 64 editions, turning *Dainik Bhaskar* into the No. 1 newspaper in 35 years.

'It's kind of fun to do the impossible,' said Walt Disney. Ramesh Chandra thought so too.

Life, the chapter between birth and death, he lived to the fullest.

And he truly believed, 'If the dream is big enough, the problems don't matter. Therefore, dream big'. Even at the pinnacle, his aspirations for DB, like life itself, were work-in-progress.

But he also nursed another fond fantasy and he being the chosen one, was around to see that come alive too.

Chapter 5

THE HOUSEHOLDER

'Every family is beautiful but ours is my favourite'

—ANON

30 November 1944 had to be a particularly auspicious day with the Gods above savouring an unusually benign moment. There had to be a shower of blessings of a very divine nature for a man born on that day to see success of such magnitude, to negotiate a bumpy road strewn with land mines and hindrances, and touch the peak as the No. 1.

For a man who was fulfilling one professional dream after the other to also give time and heart to his family would seem humanly improbable.

But that was where Ramesh Chandra stood fortuitous as Sharda Devi and he created a copybook family that welcomed new entrants and new arrivals, embracing whatever changes they brought with them.

The concept of a happy and harmonious joint family—

Ramesh Chandra with Prime Minister Narendra Modi

Ramesh Chandra with Chief Minister of Madhya Pradesh, Shivraj Singh Chouhan, at a religious function

Launch event of *Dainik Bhaskar*, Indore edition, in the presence of the then Chief Minister of MP, Arjun Singh and Union Minister HKL Bhagat. Also seen is Dwarka Prasad Agarwal, Ramesh Chandra's father (extreme right)

Ramesh Chandra serving food at a social function

Ramesh Chandra in deep conversation with his oldest son Sudhir Agarwal

Ramesh Chandra in his early 20s

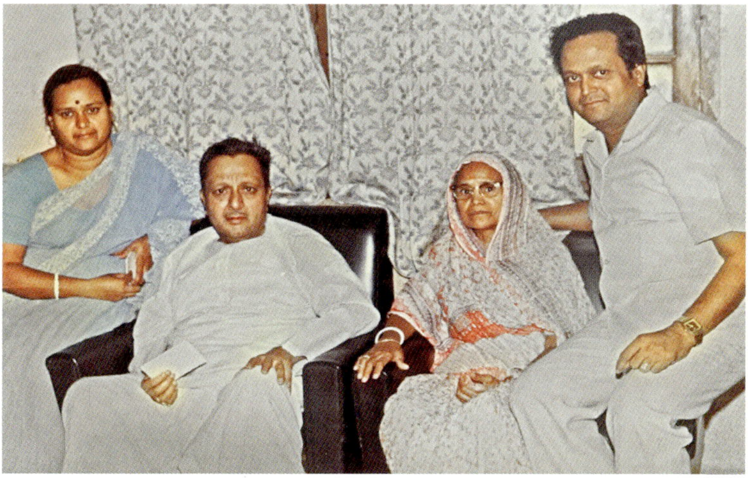

Ramesh Chandra with his father Dwarka Prasad and mother Kasturi Devi (in the middle), and sister Meena Garg

Inauguration of one of *Dainik Bhaskar's* editions, by the then Chief Minister of MP, Motilal Vora and Union Minister Vasant Gadgil

Diwali celebrations at *Dainik Bhaskar's* old office in Bhopal

A portrait of Ramesh Chandra and his wife, Sharda Agarwal

दैनिकभास्कर

भारत तथा पाकिस्तान के मध्य संयुक्त आयोग स्थापित होगा

इंदिराजी के प्रस्ताव से शाही सहमत

रंगा तथा बिल्लाकोएक घंटेतक शूली पर लटकाया गया

One of the oldest issues of *Dainik Bhaskar*

With father Dwarka Prasad (2nd from right, middle row) and members of his extended family

Ramesh Chandra with the then President of India, Dr Shankar Dayal Sharma

Ramesh Chandra at an Agarwal Samaj function

Ramesh Chandra at his desk in his office in Bhopal

A happy snapshot of Ramesh Chandra with his entire family – sons, daughters-in-law, daughter, son-in-law and his grandchildren

Ramesh Chandra with his friends in Jhansi, in his younger days

Pictures of Ramesh Chandra at his wedding

Ramesh Chandra performing Diwali pujan with
sons Sudhir, Girish and Pawan

The building in old Bhopal, where it all started

Down memory lane – Ramesh Chandra and Sharda Devi with their kids on a beach vacation

Ramesh Chandra with his mother, Kasturi Devi

Ramesh Chandra with his three sons during a family function

Ramesh Chandra with his daughter,
Bhawana and son-in-law, Vishal

Ramesh Chandra with Morari Bapu, the renowned spiritual leader and preacher

Ramesh Chandra exchanging pleasantries with Pranab Mukerjee, former President of India

On the cover of *Business India* in 2008

On the cover of *Marwar* magazine

Launch event of the Jabalpur edition, with former Prime Minister Atal Bihari Vajpayee, and former Union Ministers, Kamal Nath and Girja Vyas

At the Bhumi Pujan ceremony for construction of the *Dainik Bhaskar* office in Indore

Ramesh Chandra being felicitated by Mukesh Ambani, Chairman and Managing Director of Reliance Industries Limited

At the launch event of *Divya Marathi* in Aurangabad, with the then Chief Minister of Maharashtra, Prithviraj Chavan, Chief Minister of MP, Shivraj Singh Chouhan and Union Ministers P. Chidabaram, Vilasrao Deshmukh, Sushil Kumar Shinde, Chhagan Bhujbal and Manohar Joshi

Launch of *Dainik Bhaskar*, Punjab edition at the hands of the then Chief Minister of Punjab, Parkash Singh Badal and media baron Subhash Chandra and others

Ramesh Chandra receiving the Rajiv Gandhi Award for Journalism from politician Jyotiraditya Scindia and filmmaker Madhur Bhandarkar

Ramesh Chandra in conversation with Madhavrao Scindia

Ramesh Chandra sounding the gong on the occasion of listing of Dainik Bhaskar Group, DB Corp Ltd. at the Bombay Stock Exchange, on 6th January 2010

Ramesh Chandra with Nitish Kumar, Chief Minister of Bihar, and former Union Ministers Sushil Kumar Shinde and Lalu Prasad Yadav at the launch of *Dainik Bhaskar* Patna edition

At the launch of The Sanskaar Valley School, Bhopal in July, 2006 from (L to R) Sonia Gandhi, President of the Congress Party; Jyoti Agarwal; Jayant Lal, Principal; Ratan Tata, Chairman Tata Sons Ltd.; Shivraj Singh Chouhan, Chief Minister of MP and and Ramesh Chandra Agarwal

Ramesh Chandra with Baba Ramdev, the celebrated yoga guru, at a *Dainik Bhaskar* event

Trying his hand at golf!

In a relaxed mood during a holiday

Some happy moments with his grandchildren

The *Dainik Bhaskar* office in Bhopal

The Agarwal house in Bhopal

that rare Indian phenomenon—was close to being declared endangered as it moved towards extinction in modern times. But Ramesh Chandra had a vision. Sharda Devi, his wife for 39 fulfilling years (1965–2004), and he raised a family with such traditions, connections and celebrations that children and grandchildren became one fortified unit, bound together by unshakeable values.

In fact, DB, his other passion outside the house, leaned heavily on the existence of this support system. Ramesh Chandra became who he was because his horoscope brought Sharda Devi into his life. The abundance continued in their family life too when three sons were born as his inheritors with the propitious bonus of a loving daughter who made an unplanned appearance in their lives.

"I'm told that after Sudhir bhaiya, Papa and Mummy really wanted a girl," giggled Bhawna, their only daughter and the youngest. "Because they desired a girl so much, when they had Girish he was nicknamed Pinky. And then Pawan happened. Papa would frequently tell me that one day, he was sitting in his Indore office when someone randomly came up and told him, 'You're going to have a baby girl.' Papa told him, we've already got three sons, how long are we going to keep having children? But the man insisted, 'You're going to have a girl and your fortunes will change with her birth. I can see it on your forehead.' They had no clue at that time whether a girl or another son would be born to them but Papa did tell me that they fervently wished for a daughter."

She was christened Bhawna but called 'Gudiya' at home which translated into 'Doll', a pet name popular in many North Indian households where the daughter holds a special place in everybody's heart. Till the end of his life, Bhawna was the apple of his eye, the one who got that one extra spoonful of love from her father.

Sharda Devi and Ramesh Chandra twinned as one, they did everything together. But most of all, they shared a two-chapter ideal together. Of building a business empire brick-by-brick and grooming their children, step-by-step, to slip into their inheritance and run it without friction long after they were gone. The empire and the family were inextricably intertwined and interdependent. Neither could exist without the other. To keep the empire together as one unfragmented unit, it was imperative that the family also stay together as one committed, cohesive whole. A Hitlerian stick wouldn't effectuate it, husband and wife didn't have the temperament for it either. It had to happen holistically, voluntarily and happily. Towards this did Sharda Devi and Ramesh Chandra strive all their lives, helping each other make what seemed like a fantasy fructify as an actuality.

With father Dwarka Prasad most times in a huff in his Gwalior home, and mother Kasturi Devi, a pliant, pious lady who stayed wrapped up in her pujas for the better part of the morning and drew happiness from those around her, Sharda Devi and Ramesh Chandra raised a family pretty much as they wanted to.

They were both unswerving on two fundamentals: traditions would be followed by all of them in unison and the family would stay together undivided.

Perhaps learning from his own experience where there were areas of conflict with his father, Ramesh Chandra sealed the gaps and played the glue along with his wife to ensure that the family worked together, played together, prayed together too, and stuck together in times of celebration and dejection.

With the zest for work and newspaper deadlines the supreme concern of them all, report cards from school were relegated to an inconsequential position. An unexpected disinterest considering Ramesh Chandra was a post-graduate and, rare for her time, Sharda Devi too was a graduate. In fact, her going to college in the times that she did, had its quantum of hilarity.

"Studies were not a big deal in our house," clucked Girish, "though my father had an MA Previous in Political Science and my mother had done her BA in Literature and that too way back in the 1960s from Shivpuri, a small place in Madhya Pradesh which was near a dacoit-infested area. She would tell us that when she went to college, she was the only girl in the entire class." Her family had allowed her to go to college but Sharda Devi had requested her teacher to permit her to sit separately since it was essentially a boys' class and to allow her to leave the classroom a little before everybody else. When exiting a classroom there could be quite a bit of jostling that she wanted to avoid.

A pact sprang up between her teacher and Sharda Devi where the former would flash a signal 30 seconds before she dismissed the class for the latter to slip out. Sharda Devi had smartly pre-arranged with a couple of her friends that they would wait for her outside her class and move out together.

"But unfortunately, in our house, the family was not bothered about what we were studying or which school we went to," Girish said. "They'd perfunctorily ask, 'Are you going to a good school? Oh, that's great.' If a tuition teacher who came home recommended a school, that was considered adequate and no further enquiries were made. I ended up going to seven different schools. Once I reached Class 9, Sudhir bhaiya and I started taking the call for Pawan and Bhawna, so they didn't change as many schools as I did.

"Therefore, I never took my parents to any PTA meeting or for school admission after Class 8. In fact, I even started signing as my father on school forms and report cards," he slipped in cheekily. "My father was very cool about most things at home. Whether you got a first division or a second, it didn't bother him. He was never strict with us about eating or doing anything in a particular way. It was only when we started working that we realised there were two sides to Papa. One was the casual dad at home, the other was a man who was never casual at the workplace.

"But I have to say that about education too, he never said 'no' to anything," Girish paused to say appreciatively. "He was fine with my wanting to study further. When Pawan was in Class 11 and wanted to study abroad, we spoke to dad about it and he had no problem with it. To his credit, there was never any remark like, 'Why are so you spending so much money on sending him abroad or on his studies?' So while it's true that our joining him in the business was more on his mind than our studies, he didn't question our decisions."

'You don't choose your family. They're God's gift to you as you are to them,' said Desmond Tutu. Sharada Devi and Ramesh Chandra certainly believed in the gift they'd been bestowed with and raised their children by believing in them, confident that imparting the right values to them would carry them through.

The implicit trust didn't have a beginning, it was there, always, and continued when Sudhir and Girish were ushered into the business before they hit even 19 years of age. As documented earlier, Sudhir had started apprenticeship at 13, put in charge of Bhopal at 15 and elevated to the post of manager of the Indore arm at 19. Girish took over the Gwalior unit when he was still a schoolboy, treated like a professional, given a car and asked to run the office.

"Papa introduced me to the team, said, 'He's going to manage this place henceforth', and though I was a kid, he never once asked me about any of my expenses," Girish relished the managerial responsibility that was given to him by parents who instinctively knew that he'd rise to the occasion.

The duties that came with the privileges took away whatever sense of entitlement a schoolboy might've otherwise luxuriated in as his birthright.

Girish analysed, "If you have a car to yourself in Class 12, it could be looked at as a luxury or as a requirement. It was a necessity because I couldn't possibly go to office on a motorcycle. It's also true that even as a student, I would be invited as the Chief Guest to some function or the other because of *Bhaskar*. But one couldn't feel entitled to anything because it wasn't as if one could shirk work the next morning. I had a gruelling schedule of more than 12 hours a day. I'd go to school at 7.30 in the morning and come back at 1pm, have a quick lunch and go to office at 2.30 pm, stay there till 9.30 pm, come back, hit the sack and go back to the same grind the next day. So when friends would say, let's go to the club for a round of badminton in the evening, I'd wonder how I could do that when I was working till 9.30 pm and had to be back in school early next morning again.

"I think because of the early responsibility, the maturity came in much faster," he contemplated.

Instead of a swagger, the responsibility on young shoulders worked the other way on both Sudhir and Girish.

Intrinsically a family that shrank from flaunting itself, Girish went through a spell when he would park his car half a kilometre away from school, "And walk because I didn't want anybody in school to know that I was the *Bhaskar* guy. We inherited this nature from both our parents. And the maturity to handle things came much faster because by the time we were done with one assignment, Papa had us on to another project."

It wasn't intrusive supervision but the sons, especially the two older, had jobs on the trot that came to them with ineradicable lessons.

"Two years later, I shifted to marketing and sales and travelled countrywide, to Mumbai, Bengaluru, Delhi," said Girish. "The first time I went to Mumbai, I took a friend along and stayed at the Oberoi where I paid something like Rs 1,800 for the night. A day later, I felt I hadn't earned the right to spend like this and felt so guilty that I myself checked out and went to West End hotel next to Bombay Hospital where my father used to stay. Paying Rs 600 there seemed the right thing to do and I felt good about it. But my father never asked me why I had stayed at the Oberoi."

What a parental lecture or bouts of nagging wouldn't have wrought, unstated faith did.

"Imagine, a young 18 or 19-year-old guy with money at his disposal, could have gone astray too," Girish ruminated. "But I was not even asked what I did in the evenings, where I went, what I spent on. That kind of trust worked because I myself decided that I had work to do, so would go and grab a meal somewhere close by, and stay home or in the room quietly. The sense of responsibility came on its own."

But when one of them needed a sharp rap on the knuckle, he got it from Ramesh Chandra all right. A rebuke that was rare but so emphatic that it would live on interminably.

"This was around 1993," Girish jetted back in time. "He wanted to meet and discuss a few matters with the industry people and came along with me to Mumbai. I had the sales and marketing under control and wondered why he was wasting his time with something I had wrapped up around my little finger."

Two meetings in the morning went off smoothly till 1 pm, after which there was another one scheduled for 2 pm. The jaunty young man who was escorting his father around town decided that lunch at the fancy Khyber restaurant would be in order. Ramesh Chandra's mild protestations that they had another meeting were waved away by Girish who hailed a cab, and they went to Khyber, had a hearty meal, and cabbed it to DN Road for the next appointment. When they reached at 2.25 pm, the lady they were to meet came out and said, 'You're late. I have another meeting at 2.30, so I can't meet you now.'

"That was the one time my father really gave me a dressing down," Girish remembered. "He didn't holler but he asked me, 'Tell me, what have we come to Mumbai for? What's your priority? To eat or to work? If you wanted to eat at that restaurant, we could have gone there in the evening after completing our work and enjoyed a meal. You were so caught up with your fancy lunch that the very purpose of our visit was finished.'"

The chastened son who wanted the earth to open up and swallow him, was driven to tears. "My dad told me, 'Don't behave like an idiot, start prioritising your work'. That day's lesson has stayed with me forever," he swore.

It bears repetition here: when it came to work, the easy-going Ramesh Chandra vanished and an intent, purposeful man stood in his place.

At home or at work, Sudhir was the obedient first-born. Girish was the brat, a bit brash too, and he acknowledged it.

"Because I always had my grandfather's support, the rest of the family knew that this tattler will go with his complaints to Dadaji. And I always played that as my trump card. That made me the fearless one amongst us. So I was the only one who could pick up an argument with Mummy. Bhai was always very sober and straight. I was literally the family bully."

And Bhawna as the only female sibling bore the brunt of his browbeating that was accompanied by headstrong stubbornness. While Ramesh Chandra was petal-tender with his daughter, Girish who shared his birthday with her, cloaked his concern for her welfare with almost authoritarian inflexibility.

The only time her father who never said, 'No' to her, dithered and didn't crumble was when Bhawna wanted to go abroad to study.

"He always said, 'Go ahead and do it, *beta*,' he never really stopped any of us from doing anything we wanted. It was always, '*Dhyaan rakhna*, take care' and never, '*Nahin karna*, you can't do it.' There was never an outright 'No' from him for anything." The one exception was when Bhawna wanted to go abroad to study after Class 12. Her friends who were flying out for higher studies came from professional families. People like a professor's daughter or an IAS officer's daughter were brought up differently and their families had a different mindset. "While in our family, no girl had gone abroad to study at that time," Bhawna recalled. Ramesh Chandra didn't warm up to the idea and Bhawna too didn't push him. "If I had put my foot down or explained it to him in a better way or taken him with me to check out the campus like how it's done today, maybe he'd have been convinced. But at that time, I too didn't have any exposure to the world," she conceded.

Those were different times when Ramesh Chandra didn't entertain the idea of his only daughter going out of his vision to study.

But the one who drew the line and made rules for his sister was Girish and not the parents. The first major blow-up was over Bhawna, like Girish himself, refusing to show up at the college gate in fancy, chauffeur-driven wheels. Like her brothers, she cringed and shied away from showing off.

"I don't know how anybody else sees it but in Bhopal we were among the few who were really privileged, brought up in comfort. I didn't want to stand out in college by arriving in a big car, so I asked Papa for a scooty," Bhawna remembered.

The one who said, 'No' was of course the self-confessed family bully.

It actually came to a point where Ramesh Chandra threw up his hands and told her, 'You convince your brother and I'll get it for you.' Bhawna's counter of 'You're my father, not he,' melted Ramesh Chandra's heart enough to intercede on her behalf.

"I said I will go walking but I will not go with a chauffeur. I won't enter college in a car," she repeated. "So that's how I finally got a Kinetic Honda scooter."

She did—but on Girish's terms. Bhawna had to give it in writing that she wouldn't stay out after 7 pm and that she wouldn't have three people on the Kinetic. "He would literally call up from office for the first few days to check whether I was home before 7 pm or not," she added.

Ramesh Chandra was indulgent, especially with his daughter. "Mummy would shout a little at me saying, 'She's not doing any work in the house, how will she manage after she's married?' But dad would say, 'She'll learn when she has to.'"

It was no surprise at all that the one who wielded the stick was Girish.

"He was stricter than anybody else in the family," Bhawna merrily recounted. "The last few years before I got married, he began to insist that every single day I had to make at least one *sabzi* (vegetable), otherwise he wouldn't eat. Papa never insisted on anything like that but Girish did. One dish had to be made personally by me. My mother who doted on Girish would cajole me and say, 'Come on, make it'."

While this sibling banter went on, an everlasting piece of advice that Ramesh Chandra gave his sons was, 'Treat daughters-in-law like daughters. And take care of your sister like she's your daughter.'

Dispensing wisdom comes easily to elders in most families. Where Ramesh Chandra and Sharda Devi scored was when they showed that they could assimilate as much as they disseminated. A situation that demanded it from them arose when eldest son Sudhir met a pretty Punjabi girl from an affluent family in Delhi, and an intense romance blossomed. It was uncommon, a little unbecoming too for a traditional Vaish family of Marwaris where the father was a leading light of his society to welcome such a match in the previous millennium.

But it was a match that the heavens ordained when Sudhir went to look at a prospective bride for his closest friend Vikas Rakheja and she happened to be Jyoti's elder sister.

"I was exceptionally close to Vikas and his family, so I went with them to Jyoti's house to see her sister as a match for him," said Sudhir, still seeming a tad bashful as he flicked through the pages of his love story. "I was as good as a son to Vikas' father, so when the wedding happened, I was thoroughly involved in the arrangements, and did everything I could like a family member."

Sudhir was also exceptionally introverted. So reticent to broach the subject with his father that it was his more outgoing brother, Girish, who broke it gently to his parents.

"In our family, for generations together, there had been no inter-caste marriage. So my brother's marriage was a very big deal for my father," explained Girish who had played an exemplary part in taking Sudhir-Jyoti to the altar. "Papa was also a social worker in the Agarwal *samaj* (society). When you are a torch-bearer of a community where everybody looks up to you and your son is getting married to a girl from a different caste and culture, it is very sensitive territory to negotiate. When I told my father that Bhai wanted to marry a girl who was not a Marwari, his initial reaction was that this sort of marriages didn't happen in our famiy. But after he spoke to Sudhir, he gradually came around and said, 'If it's a question of my children's happiness, so be it.'"

That was when the stars presented a *fait accomplis* and signalled to Ramesh Chandra that this was a pre-destined, celestial match.

Ramesh Chandra understanding his son's heartbeat and accepting it wholeheartedly was evident in the wedding celebration that became the *cause celebre* of Bhopal.

The ceremonies were so spectacularly unstinted that nobody could ever charge Ramesh Chandra with holding back because his daughter-in-law hailed from another community.

That was a time when Marwaris were rather infamous for the dowry demands they made on a bride's family. But Ramesh

Chandra was a man who marched to his own beat. He wanted his daughter-in-law to come gracefully into their house in the clothes she was wearing and not stagger in with a pile of gifts from her family.

Four months after her marriage, Ramesh Chandra asked Jyoti, his 22-year-old daughter-in-law, what she did the whole day long. The reply from her was, she relaxed and did nothing between breakfast, lunch and dinner. He told her, 'Start coming to the office from tomorrow.'

"I was just out of college and didn't know the head or tail of business. But Sudhir taught me a lot and Papa was extremely supportive of everything we did."

One day, Jyoti looked at the building in front of their office and talked of wanting to start a multi-cultural centre there. "Papa never said 'No' to anything." And Abhivyakti, one of Bhopal's most vibrant, not-for-profit cultural hubs, was born. By now, Jyoti had discovered that she enjoyed being a working woman and Ramesh Chandra's approach didn't change when her daughter Shubh was born. There was no 'stay home and mind the baby' diktat.

Au contraire, Sudhir recalled that he instilled in them the need to rough it out. When Shubh was born in September 1996, they were in the throes of their crucial Rajasthan launch. "After a small function in Bhopal on the 40th day, we took the 42-day-old infant in an overnight train from Bhopal to Agra in the biting cold, got down at 5 am and drove to Jaipur. He never mollycoddled us or thought, how will they do it, this is too tough to do. He would always say, '*Ho jayega,* it will happen'."

"Papa and I were extremely close, with a different level of connectivity," said Jyoti. "I invested a lot the first two or three years in the family set-up but after that I ran the house. Papa and Mummy were very clear that I would take the decisions on weddings, jewellery, clothes, the house, everything. When I wanted to start a school, the only question Papa asked me was, how much do you need for it? I had no sense of money, we spent about Rs 60 crore on it." It was money well ploughed as The Sanskaar Valley became one of the most prestigious day and boarding schools in the whole state.

"Then four years ago, he told me to start an English newspaper. I conceived the paper from scratch, we worked on it diligently. During the launch phase of *The DB Post*, I would have to stay in the office past midnight," Jyoti recalled. "He never fussed about my timings. In fact, we reached a stage where sometimes, if he wanted to convey something to Sudhir, I became the medium between them. I can't decide whether it was Sudhir or Papa who gave me the maximum support."

As the years slipped by, the conditions too began to wear away in their severity. Jyoti slipped out of the saree and her wardrobe started making space for trousers, jeans and tees for casualwear. A day soon came when Ramesh Chandra himself looked at his daughter-in-law and wondered aloud, "I've often thought about why I imposed so many restrictions on you. I really don't know why I did it at that time." This was, once again, Ramesh Chandra adjusting his mind to a changing order and even welcoming it heartily.

The marriage of all four of their children added a new dimension to Ramesh Chandra and Sharda Devi's family.

It was Girish's turn after the launch of *Dainik Bhaskar* in Jaipur. Girish had met industrialist SK Golcha's daughter Namita, way back in 1991 at a wedding in Bhopal and had proposed to her. Interestingly, she had turned him down. So he enlisted the support of her mother who had decided that Girish was the most suitable boy for her daughter and spoke to her husband about it.

"We went to them with a formal proposal," said the industrialist from Jaipur. "Then Rameshji and Sudhirji came to Jaipur and we spoke about it."

The Golchas who were already impressed with the Agarwal family, were bowled over when Ramesh Chandra underlined his principle of not accepting anything from the bride's parents. Instead, he wanted to take Namita to Mumbai for her wedding attire and trousseau shopping. The unexpectedness of Ramesh Chandra's gesture floored the industrialist.

The Golchas were Jains, the Agarwals were Marwaris. But after Sudhir wed Jyoti, distinctions had blurred and the doors had opened for fresh thinking as Ramesh Chandra strode into the future asking only for a daughter-in-law who'd step into their house as a daughter.

Every marriage in the family had its special features. When *Dainik Bhaskar* was embroiled in a print war with *The Tribune* in Chandigarh, a well-settled family in the city had invited Ramesh Chandra over for dinner. Two years later, Ramesh Chandra wanted their daughter Nitika's hand for his third son, Pawan.

By now, he had implicit confidence in Sudhir and Jyoti's judgement.

"Papa trusted people," said Jyoti. "When Pawan was getting married, we went and finalised the girl. My in-laws didn't even meet her before the engagement. Papa remembered Nitika from the dinner in Chandigarh but Mummy hadn't even seen her."

Each daughter-in-law came from a different social space but struck up her own equations in the family. Namita's experiences filled in the colours required to paint the grand joint family portrait that Ramesh Chandra and Sharda Devi had single-mindedly framed together.

"Ours was an arranged-cum-love marriage," Namita recounted. "My mother was from Bhopal and we had all met at a wedding. So Girish and I knew each other before we got married. But I met Papa for the first time at our engagement." It was Ramesh Chandra's renowned trust in what the rest of his family had decided and going along with it.

For Namita it was a leap of faith because she came from an essentially nuclear set-up while Ramesh Chandra and Sharda Devi had planted the seeds for the growth of a large, joint family.

"I was slightly apprehensive about it," she allowed herself to disclose. "The culture and customs were different. But Papa and my mother-in-law were such simple people that it was easy to make adjustments and fit in. My father-in-law especially was so broadminded and accepting that it wasn't difficult at all."

Nitika Singhal's introduction to the family was totally different. When her father, also a well-placed businessman in Chandigarh, invited the newspaper baron from MP who was posing a challenge to *The Tribune,* home for dinner, she got her first glimpse of both her father-in-law and her husband-to-be, Pawan.

"It was a very formal dinner and the next time I met Papa was a year-and-a-half later. I am six-and-a-half years younger to Pawan, so I was studying, doing my MBA while he was already working. One fine day, Papa called my father in Chandigarh and said, 'We are keen to meet Nitika, would you like to meet us?'

"My father was very surprised to get that call from Papa after nearly two years. And Papa had only taken a perfunctory look at me at that dinner at home. But he hadn't expressed any desire to come personally and see me again. When all the three brothers and the two sisters-in-law came to meet us in Delhi, Papa had told Pawan, 'If you like the girl even 60 per cent, say 'Yes' and come back because I really liked the family and I really liked the girl.' That was it."

Both Ramesh Chandra and Sharda Devi were confident that the older siblings would know what was good for the family, and so they went along with their decisions. It was a happy phase for all of them as Bhawna also got engaged, Pawan followed suit and Jyoti-Sudhir were expecting their second child.

For Miss Singhal from Chandigarh, the transition to Mrs

Pawan Agarwal was made easy, "Because Papa made me feel so welcome in the house. They were a very loving family. Bhawna didi had also got married by then, so I was the youngest in the family and he treated me like a kid."

While the house brimming with three daughters-in-law brought a glow to his face, Ramesh Chandra also had to go through the tug of letting Gudiya, his daughter Bhawna, start a new life in a new place with a new family.

Until the right man came along, Bhawna was grateful that her father didn't push her into meeting a string of boys. "I got married at 26 and I'm sure they must have been worried about it," she stated. "But I never heard anyone in the family lament that she's not getting married, find a guy for her. I was never made to feel that I was getting on in years and was still unmarried. 17 years ago, girls got married by the time they were 21. Papa had already seen Nitika and really liked her as the right match for Pawan. But he said that only after my marriage was finalised would he ask Pawan to go and see her."

It was once again destiny that had reserved the best for Bhawna when Namita's father, SK Golcha met Vishal Agarwal, the polished, eligible son of VISA Steel founder Vishambhar Saran, and told Ramesh Chandra that this seemed like a good match for Bhawna. Vishal who had studied in Mayo College, Ajmer, went to Cheltenham in the UK and to London School of Economics before doing his Masters from Oxford. Father Vishambhar was Russi Mody's right-hand man at Tata Steel for three decades before he set up VISA (an amalgam of the first two letters from his name and that of his wife Saroj)—another self-made man like Ramesh Chandra himself.

Not only was Vishal ideal son-in-law material, he also had only a fraternal twin and a younger brother. That made it a family of three sons with Bhawna once again getting the special status of being the only girl in the set-up. It was a tailor-made fit for Ramesh Chandra's Gudiya.

The wedding was one of those occasions in a North Indian family when happiness would be palpable in tearful scenes which climaxed with sobbing during *bidaai*, the ceremony which symbolised the daughter parting from the family she was born into and stepping into a new life with her husband and in-laws.

"During my wedding, there was enough crying going on every day," Bhawna got wet-eyed at its mere recall. She left for Delhi after the *bidaai* and when she called home the next day, she was told that her father hadn't spoken to anybody since morning. Jyoti told Bhawna, "There's pin-drop silence at home that makes me realise what it's like when the daughter of the house gets married and moves out. Papa had his tea, read the papers and apart from seeing off various relatives, he hasn't spoken to anybody else."

For bridegroom Vishal, it was a whirlwind episode. He met Bhawna in February and they were wed in April. The wedding too was a big surprise. When the *baraat* (the groom's party) arrived in Bhopal, the welcome committee had no less than three Chief Ministers awaiting them with garlands.

"Yes, Digvijaya Singh (MP), Ajit Jogi (from the newly-carved state of Chattisgarh) and Ashok Gehlot (Rajasthan) were there with garlands," he laughed.

That was in April, 2002 followed by Pawan and Nitika's marriage two months later in June.

By this time, Ramesh Chandra and Sharda Devi had set the ground rules for a joint family to function on a well-oiled track. There were customs and traditions that the sons, the daughters-in-law and their children learnt to follow.

"In this family, a lot of rituals are followed whereas in my parents' home we didn't observe any," Namita recorded the adjustments she had made. "We celebrated just Diwali every year. But here, many rituals were followed, there was something happening practically every month. I got used to it gradually and easily because they were all very nice people."

Although DB Group was an inheritance only for the men in the family, her father-in-law encouraged everybody to pursue their interests.

"He was very open to the idea of all of us working. His only advice was, don't work for the money and get into a rut where that becomes your priority. The family has to come first. He would always say, 'Even if there are hard times, the family should face it together. The family should always live together, kids included.' He instilled in all of them the idea of oneness, that they should grow together as brothers and sisters, like siblings, and not as cousins. It was very important for him that everybody should be together."

The claustrophobia of such constant togetherness under one roof was consciously dissipated by Ramesh Chandra, "ensuring that everyone got his/her space to do whatever he/she wanted and by accepting each one as an individual," noted Namita.

Pawan had clarity on it.

"Papa would talk to us about it, that we were the sons of the same set of parents but our wives came from three different families. So we were always aware that there they would have different aspirations, different ambitions and one would have to give them their freedom. If you didn't give them the freedom to flourish, it would ultimately tell on the family. Papa always recognised that, and Sudhir bhaiya too."

Bhopal was the family home for everybody, irrespective of where they lived otherwise, and this was where everybody met and celebrated every festival all year around.

Girish added his thought to it.

"We are a traditional family but we are not orthodox," he commented. "We are not one of those fussy families. Bhabhi and Namita come from a very different, very liberal background. But in our family, it was not compulsion that drove us to observe festivals and rituals together, we did it and we continue to do it because we wanted to. We also realised that if we didn't follow them, the next generation would never do it. So to that extent, it was a must for all of us. Papa was easy about it but Mummy insisted on following every ritual and puja."

Namita's father remarked, "Bhabhisa (as he called Sharda Devi) was a gentle lady. But she was the one who set up strong systems at home."

Family to Ramesh Chandra did not encompass only his children and their spouses. "He would say, we are five families in one. For him, Jyoti bhabhi's family, Nitika's family, Vishal's family and mine were all included in his private universe. He would always say, if anything happens in any of these families, we have to be there," Namita expounded. "It extended not only to functions but also to solving issues. For example, in my family, my father and brother were not getting along, so Papa played the mediator. He talked to both of them and the best part was that even my brother, though he's so young, could relate to him. Papa was so forward in his thinking that all age groups were at ease with him."

"Yes, he cared more for my family than anyone in my own family did," endorsed Namita's father. "When there was a bit of a crisis in my family, he stood by me all the way and had instructed Girish and Namita to leave everything else, make sure Golchaji is comfortable and try to sort it out.

"Namita told me that Rameshji would always tell them, our family is not just six of us, it includes the families of all my daughters-in-law. All of you must have as much respect and regard for their families as you have for our family. In today's world it is very rare to come across anybody else who has such a strong sense of family bonding."

But life didn't narrowly revolve only around, 'Me, my wife, my kids, my family'. 'There must be *hariyali*, greenery and prosperity all around us,' was one of his mottos. When that principle combined with his boundless energy, his quest for new knowledge and his insatiable hunger for more, it resulted in Ramesh Chandra looking around and extending his hand to all those he cared for.

For Dr Vinod Goyal who married youngest sister Neelam, Ramesh Chandra Agarwal had ceased to be a brother-in-law years ago. "We had become friends. He helped me in every way possible," said Dr Goyal who set up an eye hospital. And, like most others in whom Ramesh Chandra was personally invested, Goyal too got that daily phone call at 10 pm for years without fail. All Ramesh Chandra would ask him was, '*Haan, Vinodji, aur boliye?* What's happening?' Even if the doctor wasn't inclined towards business, his brother-in-law had a fine sense of how much the practice could grow and how to achieve it.

"I only knew how to be a good doctor. But today huge investments are required for a good hospital. He combined the medical practice with his business sense," reported Vinod.

It was Ramesh Chandra who suggested that they would stand to benefit from it if Neelam got out of the kitchen and ran the administrative side of the hospital. She had the bloodline of the Agarwals with a natural flair for business. "It was the turning point of my business," attested Dr Goyal as the husband and wife team turned the hospital into a winner.

Ramesh Chandra also shared with Goyal one of the mantras that drove him. 'If something has to be cracked and it requires 100 kilos to break it, even 99 kilos won't do it, you will have to apply 100 kilos to do it.' It was Ramesh Chandra's way of saying that you can achieve what you want only if you give it your 100 per cent. Nothing less will do.

Going into the solvent business was another sterling example of Ramesh Chandra's inclusiveness. Girish said expansively, "My Mama (mother's brother) knew the edible oil business, so Papa started the solvent business with him."

Mahendra Garg, his uncle who knew the oil trade, prospered in the solvent business as did Ramesh Chandra who drew satisfaction from watching the *'hariyali'* sprout around him.

Another Mamaji, Vishnu Garg also recalled the close association he had with his brother-in-law and media baron who never had his nose in the air.

"When he'd come to Gwalior, he'd happily eat his favourite *chaat* from street carts, never conscious of his social status.

"We did a some work together on DB Mall in Gwalior which was beset with legal problems," added Vishnu Garg. "I had bought the land but it had so many complications that I stepped back from it. Rameshji confidently saw it through and built the mall."

"Papa kept helping out people," Girish remarked. "He had a friend in Bhopal who said, 'Let's set up a steel plant together,' and my father did it with him. He set up a cement plant with someone else. My dad toiled over it but had to close it down. He made a lot of mistakes too. He must have burnt his fingers many times in various businesses and he must have been let down by people on several occasions. But that never stopped him from trusting people."

"There was something to learn from him each day. He would never carry his success or failure around. He'd put it behind him and say, 'Fine, now let's keep working.' His hobby was work and the rest of his time was reserved for family, for mummy and all of us. But," Bhawna added thoughtfully, "I think he enjoyed his grandkids more than his own kids."

Whatever the partnerships he struck in his life, Ramesh Chandra's most inviolable partnership was with his wife Sharda Devi.

"Papa had a terrific connection with Mummy," said Girish. "They would travel together. I remember my mother and father had toured America, Japan and Europe, way back in the 1980s and 90s.

"Both of them were also very socially inclined. He was always grounded and so was she. There used to be a movie called *Shriman Shrimati* starring Sanjeev Kumar and Raakhee. It was about a couple that would go around resolving other people's issues. I used to joke with my parents that they were like *Shriman Shrimati* as they would spend much of their time sorting out the problems in some family or the other. I would always ask them, 'What've we got to do with any of their squabbles?' But they would tell me, 'You won't understand it now, son.'"

Sharda Devi knew her husband inside out and since Ramesh Chandra was never inclined to splurge on himself, she did all his shopping for him and he unquestioningly wore what she bought for him.

While the year 2002 took off with much frivolity as there were two weddings in the family and another grandchild on the way, what escaped notice was that Sharda Devi's memory seemed to be blanking out. Then her eyesight too started getting cloudy. Nobody thought that an eye check-up followed by a brain scan would throw up what it did—a tumour that necessitated a second opinion from an expert in Mumbai.

At Jaslok Hospital in Mumbai, while Sharda Devi sat feeling quite healthy outside neurologist Dr Joy Desai's room, he was reading her MRI report inside where the mood was a contrast. The doctor told Jyoti that this was an aggressive, five-centimetre, Grade 4 tumour with a life expectancy of six to nine months.

"She was complaining of only a headache and here we were talking of a Grade 4 tumour with only six to nine more months of life," Jyoti recalled the traumatic medical verdict.

It made the Gujarat launch enormously poignant as, despite Sharda Devi's dire diagnosis of a malignant tumour in her brain, the family kept its chin up and moved to Ahmedabad.

By then, Jyoti who had come into the family in 1993 and Namita who followed five years later, had nestled comfortably with the norms set by Sharda Devi. The ailing mother was assured that her family was in the safe hands of Jyoti as she watched her take over the reins of the household and hold them all together just the way Ramesh Chandra and Sharda Devi had desired it to be.

"Soon after Bhawna's marriage in April and Pawan's in June, we got to know that my mother-in-law was in the last stage of brain cancer," recalled Namita. "So the next two years were very traumatic. Smack in the middle of it, we were launching *Divya Bhaskar* in Gujarat."

That was also the last time the family moved together and set up temporary residence wherever there was a launch. That one act of togetherness had to be forsaken as the children were all growing up and could no longer be shifted around.

Characteristically, when the medical report delivered that fatal news to them in August, 2002, there was a temporary reversal of roles. Like parents who shielded their children from harsh realities, the three sons and their wives protected Ramesh Chandra from the devastating truth, breaking it to him piece by piece over several months.

With Ramesh Chandra being a heart patient and highly diabetic, the family initially told him that just like he got the blockage in his heart removed with angioplasty, all she needed was surgery to remove the block in her brain.

"We never used the word 'cancer' or 'chemotherapy' in front of either Mummy or Papa," Jyoti said.

"For a long time, we didn't tell him that she had brain tumour," Namita disclosed. "This was because they were both very attached to each other. When he'd gone through tough times in his early days and he had left home with four kids ready to live in a garage, my mother-in-law had stood by him like a rock. She too had a rough time in the joint family but they went through it together, supportive of each other and weathering all storms together."

When the full import of her condition was finally conveyed to him, he was heartbroken but brave. Perhaps he had seen the signs and understood that time was running out for the companionship of a lifetime. So he echoed his sons' line of thought and agreed that they could either give it all up or continue with normal life and keep doing the best they could for Sharda Devi. The adrenaline rush of a high-decibel launch in the workplace and the anxiety over a life slowly ebbing away at home, thus ran concurrently for months—until January 2004 when Ramesh Chandra lost his life support.

"I think by then he was a bit prepared for it," Jyoti observed. "Papa being a very positive man said, 'There is a big vacuum in my life', but I think he never recovered from the fact that he no longer had his partner by his side. He was only 60 years old."

It was Meena Garg, his younger sister (to whom he apportioned a sizeable percentage of his affection) that he poured his heart out to. Making her his confidante was a by-product of their closeness.

"He always watched out for me," Meena said, touched at the memory of her only brother. "He would say, I'll always be there for you, whatever the time. When my husband had a haemorrhagic attack and I phoned Bhaisaab at 5 am, by God's grace, my brother who never answered the phone, picked it up himself at the first ring. The anxiety in my heart must have reached out and connected with him. He told me, 'Don't worry, Meena.' In 15 minutes, Pinky, Pawan and their wives had reached my house and he was admitted to hospital within ten minutes," she said gratefully.

When Ramesh Chandra lost his wife, he shared his true feelings with Meena and she was privy to some of his emotional secrets too.

"When he once had a heart problem in Delhi, he told me, 'I have asked Bhagwan for something. The children are settled,

I have everything I want, there's no shortage of anything. But Sharda has left me. I've told God that if you have some work left for me to do here, I'll do it. Otherwise I'm ready to join Sharda. Until then, I'll work for society.'"

The sibling-connect surfaced again when Ramesh Chandra had his first tryst with heart trouble.

"Once, I had a restless night and for some reason, it made me very anxious," Meena retold the incident. "As soon as I woke up, I called up Jyoti and asked her if Bhaisaab was okay. She said, he's fine, why are you enquiring about him? I told her I was uneasy for some reason. She didn't tell me that he'd had a problem and that they had done an angioplasty on him. Much later, she talked about it and said, look at the emotional bonding between brother and sister, she knew something was amiss."

Meena also partnered him in going to the cinema hall many a time. "He was so fond of seeing movies, one day he even forgot to wear his slippers in his hurry," she chortled. "He drove barefoot and almost flew the car because he didn't want to miss the movie."

She also recalled his fondness for certain dishes that she made. "As soon as we entered the movie hall, he would ask me, 'What've you brought today?' And I'd tell him, at least wait until the interval," she chuckled.

There were changes in all their lives after Sharda Devi passed on and Pawan enumerated them.

"After Mummy passed away, all of us decided to follow certain norms to be united as a family. Until 2003, we had never faced that situation. But after Mummy, it so happened that purely for business reasons, Girish went to live in Mumbai and a little later, I too shifted to Jaipur for work. Bhopal has always been the family hub but when we began to live in different cities, we realised that we were three brothers, we had a close bond, bound by blood and common parents. But our children were cousins, they were from three different parents. We sat down with Papa and pondered over how to create that close bond among them too. It was unanimously decided that it would be essential to create occasions, family occasions, throughout the year, for them to be together. Papa was very clear that whenever there was a festival or a family occasion, whatever the urgency of the business, we should set these days aside as time that must be spent together."

Just as the brothers followed a hierarchy amongst themselves with Sudhir as the patriarch and Pawan accepting his place as the youngest, their wives too kept to the pattern. "Whatever decisions Mummy used to take for the family, Jyoti bhabhi takes those now," Pawan said.

"We also recognise that everybody has a different lifestyle," he stated. "But it's not because we live in different cities that we've avoided confrontations and problems in the family. Even if we were all living together in the same house, we would have acknowledged that everybody can't be the same and respected it."

He explained how they consciously kept the family together. "It's not just Diwali, we're all together on at least 10 occasions every year. Ram Navami, Holi, Rakhi, Navratri, Dussehra, Diwali, New Year's and my parents' birth anniversaries are all spent together. On 16 February, Mummy's birth anniversary we hold a religious discourse. On Papa's, we observe a Prerna Diwas, which is an annual social event in Bhopal. We mark these occasions in our calendars."

As the family grew larger, one seven-day holiday where even Ramesh Chandra's nonagenarian mother Kasturi Devi came along in her wheelchair with her attendant and her spunk, got pencilled into the annual calendar.

"Earlier, we didn't do such holidays," observed Bhawna. "We did a few religious trips to places like Kedarnath and Badrinath. But after Mummy passed, we made sure that Papa and Dadi were with us on all our trips."

For parents who had at one time ruled that Jyoti should make the 7 am tea for everybody, Ramesh Chandra evolved 180 degrees. He reached a space where he not only admired Jyoti's management efficiency whether she showed it in the way she ran Abhivyakti and Sanskaar Valley School or in the manner she stepped in and took care of the entire family, he even once questioned her when he found her in the kitchen. 'Why are you wasting your time doing something that the staff can manage?' he asked her. It displayed a man who was practical, flexible and capable of accepting that change was a constant.

By the time Nitika joined the family, equations had undergone a sea-change. "I was the daughter who could say anything to him," said Nitika. "He was such fun and he was a bit scared of me too. Because he was diabetic, I was like a little mother to him. I'm the fitness freak in the family. So Papa would get scared seeing me because I'd start nagging and saying, 'Papa, please go for a walk.' He was just so easy to be with. Papa never said, 'No' to me for anything. Never. And he would constantly tease Pawan by asking him, 'Is Nitikaji giving you anything to eat?' That was because I used to control everybody's diet." He'd exhort her too to eat better and say in jest, 'Eat or people will say Ramesh Chandra doesn't feed his daughters-in-law properly.'

Like her two sisters-in-law, Nitika too had tales of how easily he adjusted to life with everybody around. "I don't think I have ever met anybody like Papa," she said enthusiastically. "Whatever you suggested, he was game to do. Let's go to a movie, let's go out for dinner, let's go to Mumbai, let's have only toast for dinner. He was fine with anything. Small things like his clothes not being ironed on time, things which could irritate a man after Mummy not being there, never evoked a reaction from him. At his age and at the level at which he was, he was so easygoing, he could even wear an un-ironed kurta and go out for dinner."

Nitika also presented her father-in-law with something so precious that it teared him up.

"Mummy was really unwell and she passed away when I was five months pregnant," she said. On 8 May, her daughter Miraya was born.

"I very clearly remember when I was coming out of the OT after having a Caesarean baby, Papa was standing outside and he had tears in his eyes. He told me, 'You've brought Sharda back to me,' because 8 May was their wedding anniversary. A girl child on the same date was so beautiful."

There was something karmic happening because two years later, her son Kushaan was born on 20 August—sharing his birthday with Sudhir Uncle.

Nitika also recalled how they'd get a whiff that he was about to pull somebody's leg. "Whenever he wanted to tease any of us, he would call us, Nitikaji or Pawanji, Mirayaji, Kushaanji. Whenever he'd join 'ji' to your name, you knew he was going to pull your leg over something."

The days when he was reluctant to send Bhawna out to study were also relegated to history when he was proud to see Sudhir and Jyoti's daughter Shubh fly to Singapore and then to the US to study, setting into motion the new practice of all the Agarwal kids, irrespective of gender, going wherever they wished to study or work.

Being Ramesh Chandra also meant that his house received a stream of visitors, some high-profile ones too. "But the really beautiful part was that whether it was an acquaintance or a celebrity, whether it was Sadhguru, Amma, Ravi Shankar or Shivraj Singh Chouhan, he treated everybody in the same manner. The house was never in a tizzy because a VIP was coming over,"remarked Nitika.

He'd spare no expense—or question anybody's expense account—when it came to his family. But splurging on himself was never on the cards.

"Despite being such a tremendously successful man, he wouldn't think twice before getting into a train if he had to," commented Girish. "He was so grounded. He would never kick up a fuss and insist on travelling only by plane or that he had to fly only first class. He also didn't care for brands. About 10 years ago, I was told that Patek Philippe was the best watch around, so I bought him one. But I had to literally cajole him into wearing it. A few days later, when his assistant called up to say the watch had stopped, I had to explain to him that this was a quartz, if he kept it aside for three days and didn't wear it, he'd have to shake it to start it. That it had to be wound regularly. My father was like, 'What kind of watch is this that you pay eight to ten lakh rupees for it and it stops working? My Titan watch works better.' My sister gave him another watch that was one-tenth the price and he liked that more than the Patek Phillippe," laughed the slightly more flamboyant son.

The patrimony received by Ramesh Chandra's legatees was thus hugely more than a sturdy, throbbing, widespread business. For among their many inheritances was the keenness to emulate the social good that their parents had quietly left behind.

"There were so many people Papa and Mummy helped in different ways, something that even we were unaware of,"said Bhawana. Papa used to say, 'God has given me a little extra for a reason. If I'm not able to fulfill that reason and help people, then why did He give it to me?'"

As Bhawna had earlier observed, his greatest joys were his grandchildren—he was too preoccupied with empire-building to spend quality time with his own children but experienced that euphoria by bonding with his grandchildren. They too knew how to wrap him around their little finger.

"When all of us were in the Maldives for a family holiday and we went snorkeling," recorded Bhawna, "Papa didn't want to go into the sea because he didn't know swimming. So Vivaan (her son, the youngest grandchild) also said, 'I'll stay with Nanu' and refused to go into the water." At that time, Shourya knew just how to handle him. "Baba," he told his grandfather, "You've taken so many major risks in your life but you're afraid of such a small one?" Egged on by Shourya's well-timed prodding, he took the plunge.

"And he loved what he saw underwater," Bhawna broke into a smile at the recollection. "Seeing him, Vivaan also got into the water."

But reaching that state of bliss with the family didn't happen overnight, it took years for Ramesh Chandra to really return to hearth and home after he lost the companion who had shared his highs and sighs and had been his co-architect in the building of their family nest.

The death of his wife's brother which happened one year later, dealt him another blow.

"My father had the vision, while my Mamaji (Uncle) ran the solvent business and managed it completely," Sudhir said. "He was also setting up a plant in Sri Lanka and my father had great ambitions for it. He would say, if it does well, I'll increase the capacity by five times and so on and so forth. But my uncle died in a tragic car accident there in Sri Lanka. The factory was set up but it never went into production. After that accident, my father's heart was not in it and he sold it."

The four children were living with their own grief of losing their mother, unaware of just how the tragedy and loneliness would hit their father, the sorrow manifesting itself in ways unimaginable to his family. It led to an alarming stage where he seemed to lose interest in all that he'd built so assiduously—the business, the family—he seemed to withdraw from it all.

Since that phase was put behind them and Ramesh Chandra had returned rejuvenated, Girish talked of it clinically.

"My father was doubly upset when my uncle died and the

solvent business went into a loss. Quite a big loss, actually. Somewhere, Dad began to lose interest in the business and in working the way he used to. There came a time when he stopped going even to the office which was unimaginable for anybody who knew Papa and his passion for work. He changed his whole system of functioning. He would operate from home, get up at any time, sleep again. We thought it was okay, if his heart wasn't in his work, so be it."

For a man who was eternally on the go, Ramesh Chandra began to pull back from the world he had created and, one day, said like a man demoralised, 'I get the feeling that my style of working has become outdated, the market has changed. I used to work fearlessly with a lot of courage and conviction in myself and everything used to fall into place. I would take huge risks and pull them off. Now I'm unsure to what extent I should take it on.'

If this was an unexpected change in Ramesh Chandra's go-getting personality, brought on by unexpressed grief and the loneliness that had hit him harder than his family had imagined, there was a sharp U-turn once again in 2015 when he bounced back regenerated, revitalised and totally refreshed. It was like Ramesh Chandra had met the man who had feistily conquered MP, Rajasthan and Chandigarh and drawn inspiration from him.

Sometime in 2015-16, half-a-dozen years after they'd got listed on the stock exchange and become DB Corp, the family wondered if it was time for them to go on an expansion spree again. They'd grown in their stock worth but hadn't exhibited their native exuberance for a very long time.

But times had changed and this was the era of consultants. So a host of top consultant firms trooped in to study and recommend their next move.

"All the consultants suggested that there was no point doing 5 to 10 things, it was better to focus on the one or two core businesses that we had. Papa had amazing loads of energy and he wanted to have a go at everything, FMCG, real estate, do it all," Girish verbalised his flashback.

"But when all the consultants said the same thing, he came around to agreeing that we concentrate on what we were already doing."

It was at this time that going back to Gujarat firmed up in Ramesh Chandra's mind. "We had a pattern of having a family meeting once a month and at one particular meeting that we had in Bhopal, Papa flared up quite unusually," Sudhir remembered. "So at that particular meeting in Bhopal, an argument ensued over Gujarat. He said, 'You people have given up and sat back on Gujarat which had a great potential for growth.' We countered that we had tried everything in Gujarat, how much could we do there? We argued heatedly with him that day until he said, 'Okay, I'll handle the revival, the resuscitation of Gujarat.'

"I tried to talk him out of it," Sudhir admitted. "I reminded him bluntly, 'Papa, you haven't worked on the ground for nearly 10 years.' But once he'd decided, he was determined and adamant that he would take up going back to Gujarat as a challenge. He said he would devote 10 days a month to turning around our figures in Gujarat. The head office was in Ahmedabad but he said, 'I'll operate from Surat.' He told us, 'What can you do in Ahmedabad where everybody comes to you and salutes you because you are the No. 1 there? We're No. 3 in Surat, that's where we should work and bring it up.'"

Pawan added, "He was so excited that he called up my sister and told her, 'Your brothers have given me a job.'"

"We really thought it was a temporary flash of his old obstinacy, that 'I'll show you I can do it,' streak in him," the straight-talking Girish said. "We said to ourselves, 'Give him a week or two and he'll be back.' But the next thing we heard was that Papa became very serious about Gujarat. He was visiting

Gujarat 10 days a month. He was going all over and we said, 'Hey, what's happened to Papa?' He'd magically reverted 100 per cent to his old self."

At subsequent meetings, he reported on the corrections he'd made in their Gujarat operations and told his sons, 'You guys are gullible idiots, people there were mis-informing you, and you were sitting here letting them do that to you.'

Sudhir recalled with admiration, "The new systems he set up in Gujarat were so practical, doable and successful that we implemented them for the rest of India too."

It was like the rebirth of Ramesh Chandra who'd banished himself from active work for nearly a decade.

"He actually turned around whatever little he could do in those four months in Gujarat and laid the foundation for the entire state," Girish recorded their amazement at his renewed energy. "We were shocked but we also knew that Papa's detailing would be intricate, he'd prise every bit of data out of everybody."

Sudhir recollected his father's joy. "He started travelling all over Gujarat and he was super excited about it. He called up my Uncle and said, 'Vishnu, I've got a job once again. You wait and see. I'll show them that I can do it.' He would tell us, you guys hit singles but I hit only fours."

One of the many lessons imparted by Ramesh Chandra was that a time comes in one's life when one doesn't work for the money anymore, one works for the sheer passion. And he lived out his last few years passionate about everything he did which included taking care of himself and his appearance.

It was a rejuvenated Ramesh Chandra with a spring in his step and a song on his lip who took on Gujarat again.

'Never be afraid to start over. It's a chance to rebuild your life the way you wanted all along.' He knew no fear as he re-traced his steps to Gujarat, involved himself with societal events in Bhopal that gave him pleasure and decided to reboot his reserves of enthusiasm every which way.

Sudhir reported what the world around him witnessed, "Papa got involved with *Bhopal Utsav* which used to be dependent on donations for over 20 years. It is a trade fair kind of annual event. Unimaginably, once Papa went on board, he turned even that *mela* around and made it profitable with reserves of Rs 10 crore."

Girish illustrated what he saw. "Papa worked for a *gaushala* (cow shelter), he got involved with CSR activities and did a fantastic job everywhere. For various reasons, he had gone limp and inactive for almost six years, but the way he came back in the final years of his life, he seemed like a man on fire."

Was it, as it turned out, the last flicker?

Chapter 6

BHASKAR & SONS

'To live in the hearts of those we leave behind us is not to die'

—THOMAS CAMPBELL

It was like a farewell party. But nobody foresaw what it was going to be. Sometime in January 2017, when Morari Bapu, the renowned Hindu spiritualist whose nine-day-long religious discourses on *Ramcharitmanas* had to be booked and planned more than a year in advance, suddenly had his diary free from the end of March to April, and the dates went to Ramesh Chandra Agarwal rather unexpectedly.

13 years ago, a little after his wife had lost her battle to cancer, Ramesh Chandra had organised similar a *katha* or *pravachan* (discourse) with Morari Bapu and had felt peace and calm sweep over him. More than a decade later, when he wanted to have another session with him, he told Jyoti, "Family weddings get over so fast. Within three days the festivities come to an end. But when there's a *katha,* the whole house comes alive for a good 10 days."

But Morari Bapu's diary was choc-a-bloc until somebody else's booking was unexpectedly cancelled and the much-sought-after spiritualist could divert those dates to the Agarwals.

Organising an elaborate and spectacular event like Morari Bapu's *katha* in three months was a challenge. But Ramesh Chandra was in peak form and he knew that he could lean on his children to pull it off like a spiritual carnival.

"There was never any discussion about how we'd make arrangements for so many people for nine days," said Jyoti, as they simply went to work to make it a memorable programme for Bhopal city and for all those who were dear to them either by blood or close bonds.

Ramesh Chandra himself sprang a surprise on his family. "He told us, I'll sit for as long as I can, I won't be able to stay there all the time. But miraculously, he was so charged that he would be the first one to reach the venue with Man Friday Hemant Jha. And, sitting right in front, he would listen to Bapu's entire session morning and evening, every single day," Jyoti marvelled at the way her father-in-law was in an unusually ecstatic state right through the nine-day uplifting event. "His energy and enthusiasm were really amazing. He was alert and he keenly listened to every word that Bapu spoke. Surprisingly, although there were chairs, he sat on the ground all through without any problem. For someone who wasn't sure of being there for all the sessions, he would listen to the *katha*, meet Bapu in the evening, go back to the ground and greet all the guests. He was in top form and animated all through. On the last day, Bapu called Papa and gifted him the Ramayan."

That was on Wednesday, 5 April 2017.

"During the entire duration of the *katha*, Morari Bapu and his staff stayed with us in our home. Since there was a shortage of rooms, Papa suggested that his mother be shifted to his room. And so, perhaps for the first time in decades, Papa actually slept in the same room as his mother for all nine days of the *katha*," recalled Jyoti wistfully. "Papa had requested us to shift her to his room.

"Papa had invited everybody we knew for the *katha*," she added. "He called all his relatives and insisted that they come at least for a day or two. It was quite astonishing that everybody he called did come and spend time with him."

"It was almost like a *shaadi* (wedding) happening in the family," Bhawna said. "He was so happy that he was meeting everybody, sitting with the people he was close to and listening to the *katha*, eating together. People would drop in to meet Bapu. It really brought a glow to Papa's face."

"Morari Bapu stayed with us in our house those nine days with his assistants. Everybody, all our uncles, aunts, my parents, Namita's relatives, Nitika's parents, everybody was there," commented Jyoti. "Even Shubh who was studying in the US came down. It was just destined that everybody would be together with Papa."

The *katha* itself went off with consummate perfection. Nitika recalled,"We had erected a *pandal* at a stadium which could accommodate 10,000 people comfortably. Morari Bapuji's *kathas* are like that, thousands of people come to hear him.

"The *katha* wound up after the morning session on 5 April. Pawan and I were moving to Delhi the same evening because our kids were starting school. Bapuji left at 2 pm and our flight was in the evening. All of us were feeling low about leaving Bhopal; we'd lived there for six years with Papa. In the evening, only a few of us were left, we sat around having tea before our flight when Papa came out of his room, took out his *rudraksh mala* (a string of holy beads) and put it around Pawan's neck. It was the first time I'd seen Papa do something like that. I knew he was upset because he just left after that."

Next Wednesday, the same lawns where family and friends had sat around chatting and bonding, were awash with mourners in white.

One week after the *katha*, on Wednesday, 12 April 2017, Ramesh Chandra alighted from an Indigo flight from Delhi and collapsed on the last step of the escalator at the Sardar Vallabhai Patel International Airport in Ahmedabad, never to wake up again.

The *katha* that turned out to be his well-attended farewell party was not the only reason for his family to rejoice that he went a happy man. Ramesh Chandra was also a refreshed, rejuvenated man who died with his boots on.

'It's not the years in your life but the life in your years that counts,' as eloquent American lawyer and politician Adlai E Stevenson famously said. Ramesh Chandra had made every one of his 72 years count before he took the last step on that escalator with only Hemant Jha a few paces behind.

"I was with Sahib since 2005," recalled a grief-stricken Hemant. "I did everything for him. I packed his bags, took care of all his food, his medicines." Ramesh Chandra was a highly insulin-dependent diabetic. So an insulin pump would also go into the luggage wherever he went.

Hemant knew what his boss could eat or would eat, so at parties too, Ramesh Chandra would tell his host, 'Hemant will get my food for me, don't bother.'

"Sahib also communicated everything through me," said Hemant. "Whether he wanted to talk to somebody or get his ticket done, I would talk to the operator or to his office and get it done."

Hemant had reason to grieve for a boss who wore, "whatever I packed and took out for him to wear," and scolded him only once in his lifetime, "right at the beginning when he missed a flight because I couldn't wake him up on time."

That Wednesday when Ramesh Chandra collapsed in Ahmedabad on arrival, Hemant didn't ever imagine that it would be the end of his ideal world too. "Once before, because of his diabetes, his blood sugar had fallen low, his arms and legs had gone limp in Delhi. He was taken to Max hospital by Bharatji (Dr Bharat Agarwal) where he was revived and was soon okay."

Hemant had no reason to think that 12 April was any different.

"Before we went to the airport, he had seen off Pawan bhaisaab's children to school in Delhi. The flight was slightly delayed, so he had some juice at the airport. We had taken the Indigo flight from Delhi to Ahmedabad where he was in the emergency row and I was in the row just behind.

"On the flight he ate Patanjali noodles and listened to music with earphones on. As soon as we landed, he said, we'll go straight to the office. At the end of the escalator, he just sat down. I realised it was serious, that's why I called the doctor, Bharatji first. He asked me to check his blood sugar. I used to always carry all his medicines, his blood sugar test machine, everything with me. I checked his sugar, it was fine. Bharatji said, take him to Apollo Hospital.

"He never had security guards around him. He only had a follow-car wherever he went, so two cars were waiting at Ahmedabad airport to take him to the office. I put him in the car and called Jyoti bhabhi. We reached the hospital in 10 minutes. By the time we reached, the doctors were waiting for him. Maybe because of the machines there seemed to be a sign of revival, but he had already gone.

"He went too early in life," he said sadly.

A Learjet aircraft with DB emblazoned on its side stood fuelled and ready for take-off like a crisply alert employee waiting to receive his boss. After a meeting at the Ahmedabad office, Ramesh Chandra was to fly out to various places in Gujarat.

But, as Girish, ever hands-on, flew from Mumbai to Ahmedabad, the airport looked solemnly different. The bustle of the morning has been replaced by the hush of mourning.

At 3 pm, an air ambulance stood serenely on the tarmac as if in contrast to the buoyancy of the morning. With a heart laden with grief, it took off with Ramesh Chandra's body in its belly, carrying him on his final flight to Bhopal, his beloved hometown.

One of Ramesh Chandra's grandchildren broke down when she saw Hemant press his boss' legs long after he was no more and was lying peacefully in his Bhopal house. "Yes, I did that," Hemant said. "Whenever he was tired, I used to press his legs."

"It was Hanuman Jayanti a day before he passed," noted Manmohan Agarwal, unwittingly drawing the link which Ramesh Chandra's mother had always referred to.

For Kasturi Devi, his 90-plus mother, her loyal Hanuman had gone away. The lady who had seen emotionally disturbing times in her life, could only say, "He touched my feet and went, and he never came back. He's gone away, *Bhagwan ke paas* (to God)."

She referred to him as Bade (the eldest) and remembered enough to recall how loyally he'd stood by her all his life. "Bade never got angry, his father was a very angry man," she said before commenting that his hard work and good luck had paid off handsomely in his lifetime. "*Itna bhagyavan tha* (he was so blessed) that he gradually got a car, a bungalow and other things."

"I'm so happy that I was there," exclaimed Shubh. "I literally flew in for just five days. For me it was unreal. I went back to the US on 7 April, I had an exam on the 10th and on the 11th (12th in India), I got a call that Baba had passed away. It seemed like I was destined to come and spend a really good time with him for that one week. If I hadn't come down for it, I'd have never forgiven myself.

"It did seem like an unplanned farewell for him because he met all the people who mattered to him. He ended his life on a very high note. He was in the best of health, best of relationships, best mood, best at work, everything was perfect."

When the DB Chairman, a man who could've floated an airline of his own, unassumingly travelled on an Indigo flight, bid adieu in such an unforeseen manner, the first person Hemant had reached out to was Dr Bharat Agarwal.

However, even the doctor who was so close to him and was acquainted with his medical condition, hadn't see it coming. "Because his angiography was reasonable, we were just not prepared for it," Agarwal detailed why the Chairman's death was such a shock to all of them. "The last checkup and angiography that was done a few months earlier at Lilavati Hospital by Dr Mathew himself, didn't show any problem which required a stent. (Dr Mathew Samuel Kalarickal, known as the father of angioplasty in India.) We thought he would have another good 10 years. We could have done an angio for him every six months because he was so receptive to it. Yes, one can put stents in a number of times, they are biodegradable and he himself was very supportive of it. He never wanted to go for a bypass as long as angioplasty was delivering what he needed. With angioplasty, one knows that there's still scope for a bypass which is the final resort."

Eternally positive, Ramesh Chandra had taken the many rounds of angioplasty in good humour.

"When I got his first angioplasty done, he was astonished to find me standing next to him and talking. Anesthesia is not given during this procedure. The patient is fully conscious and we are always interactive and talking to him. When it was completed in about an hour-and-a-half, he came out excited because his energy levels, his working capacity, everything had noticeably gone up. He would recommend it to everybody saying, 'It's like whitewashing your house. Once a year, go and get your coronaries cleaned up. It's not a big deal.'"

Ramesh Chandra also had a lucky escape when he was in

Delhi to catch a flight to Cleveland via New York with Bharat. All appointments had been scheduled well in advance for a repeat checkup and angioplasty in Cleveland where he had undergone the procedure a few years earlier.

"It was a Sunday," Bharat remembered, "when I got a call that Rameshji had severe chest pain. An emergency angio was performed and a clot removed from the thrombus, right there in Delhi. Thank God, whatever happened was on the ground and nothing untoward happened in mid-air," he sighed with relief.

It was a life marked with many such fortunate happenings which wrapped up, typically, when he was at a happy peak.

Happiness also reigned supreme because he had handed over the running of his empire to his three sons and had the satisfaction of seeing them bond and work together as one.

In his lifetime, Ramesh Chandra had noted with satisfaction, "Sudhir has polished his two younger brothers even better than I could have and has given them independent responsibilities at the appropriate juncture. I have seen my three sons running the business together. I have seen that when Sudhirji wanted his younger brothers to carry out a responsibility, he would give his opinion and conveniently disappear at the time of taking the decision. I am happy that the three brothers have developed signals and mannerisms between them where they can share things with one another without exchanging even a single word. They have developed this chemistry on their own."

It was the Power of Three that a fortunate father saw at work—at the workplace and in their residential zone.

The Power of Three, symbolised by the Celtic pattern 'triquetra' that shows the centre of three connected circles, has had its importance since time immemorial. It has always been believed, both in Western and Eastern philosophies, that the combination of three entities yields a result far greater than just three times the power.

The Holy Trinity (Father, Son and Holy Spirit); Body, Mind and Soul; the ABCs; The Three 'R's—Reading, Writing and Arithmetic; 1,2,3; Three Blind Mice; Three Musketeers; Three Stooges; 3 Idiots and Huey, Louie and Dewey (Quack, Quack, Quack), are but simple examples of the magic of the number. "Number Three is playful, it's inspirational," said Hans Decoz, the author of *Numerology: Key to your Inner Self.* "It's a happy-go-lucky number, very optimistic. I nickname it the 'sunshine number'."

A terrific trio, unbeatable when united.

Sudhir—the natural patriarch, grounded with a built-in computer in his brain

Girish—outgoing, outspoken, the go-out-there-and-get-it-done guy

Pawan—the tech-savvy youngest, happy to look up to and be guided by those older than him

Happily, for the DB family, with one son and daughter each, the trinity of Sudhir-Girish-Pawan had the third generation of Shourya-Arjun-Kushaan and Shubh-Diva-Miraya lined up, perhaps as the next upholders of the Power of Three.

That was Ramesh Chandra's biggest legacy—leaving DB in the united hands of sons who functioned as one.

Incredibly, everybody in and around the family had noticed it because it wasn't fluke luck at work. Ramesh Chandra had consciously planted the seed of oneness in his inheritors and nurtured it in his lifetime.

"When he died suddenly, my only thought was, 'Oh God, I hope the business survives, I hope the family doesn't break up,'" observed retired bureaucrat Pradip Baijal, without mincing his words. "I have dealt closely with the Mukesh and Anil Ambani dispute, I was advising on it and I'd been a director with Patni Computers where three brothers fought intensively with each other. The company was destroyed and ultimately had to be sold."

He added that this was a situation peculiar to India because, "In other countries, you don't have family industries. I have dealt with a number of these cases. The Mittals, Pramod and Lakshminivas, also fought with each other. Family disputes destroy companies in India.

"I'm writing a book on Deng (Xiaoping, the paramount leader of the People's Republic of China who led his country after Mao). He was fascinating, he kept all the diverse leaders of China in one room and was able to go ahead. Mrs Gandhi was like that. On a smaller scale, Mr Agarwal was also like that. He was able to hold people together. It's a great quality. Mr Agarwal was a visionary who kept the flock together."

Former Chief Minister of MP Digvijaya Singh said with sadness, "I never expected Rameshji to go so soon. He was in fairly good health. In fact he spoke to me three days before this happened. He said, whenever I'm in Delhi next, we must meet, and I said, sure.

"But I'm very happy that all his three sons are carrying on the legacy of Ramesh Chandra Agarwal, I'm sure they'll keep the DB flag flying."

If the family avoided the pitfall of a division like the bitter ones seen in several other leading business houses, Digvijaya reasoned, "They also lost their mother fairly early. Therefore, I think there's stronger bonding between the brothers."

Personal friend Vivek Aggarwal, the brilliant, no-nonsense IAS officer, Principal Secretary to the Government of MP, mourned, "I miss him a lot. I took a lot of advice from him on official matters as well. And he was good fun to interact with. Though he was a generation senior to me, I never felt the gap.

"The values of the family are intact," he said, commenting on the legacy that kept the DB flag fluttering without fumbling. "In every family, if one person takes the responsibility, they don't break. I see Sudhir and Jyoti doing that. During his lifetime itself, Rameshji had given the reins of his business to his sons, especially to Sudhir. But he maintained his say in the business till the end and they always respected his views."

Stock market veteran and former Chief Investment Strategist at Reliance Capital, Madhu Kela who looked upon Ramesh Chandra as a father figure pointed out, "With the kind of systems he put in place, Rameshji gave them all important roles to play, and he instilled in them the importance of work. In life you'll be known by the work you do. Watching other families make mistakes, he definitely learnt from them what not to do. He was always learning from everywhere. He discussed this and other subjects, many times with me. Basically, he was a family man, very proud of his sons, and keen to keep them all together. It was clearly on his mind. And the sons are doing him a great favour by making sure they stay together. Sudhir is an exceptional person, so grounded, *hawa mein kuch nahin* (no kite flying), detail-oriented."

Ramesh Chandra's death was such a shock, "That I didn't have the courage to go to his funeral. I was in the US when it happened but I couldn't have seen it," said Subhash Chandra.

The media baron also noted that while other big-surname families had succumbed to a split, "It hasn't happened in this family which is a good thing. And I don't see it happening either. Because Sudhir is not only a good leader, he also knows the dharma of an elder brother. When he as the eldest brother is ready to sacrifice, the others also rally around."

Retired IAS officer and the present Chief Election Commissioner of India, Sunil Arora put it briefly. "They have always been very united. It's their *sanskaar* (cultured upbringing) which is the bedrock of a family's values."

Kamal Nath, CM of MP, knew them intimately enough to analyse, "His sons were a big asset to him. In his lifetime, he had started withdrawing from the business. So when he passed away suddenly, it didn't affect the DB Group. He had already installed people in key positions and had more or less withdrawn. They were not installed due to the circumstances, they were installed with a plan in place much before he died. So that made a lot of difference."

He saw the togetherness as, "Harmony in the family of which he was the architect. He recognised the strengths of each of his children and did division of work in his lifetime itself."

"He had a knack of understanding people thoroughly and objectively and he knew who was capable of what," underscored another close family friend, OP Rawat, former Chief Election Commissioner.

"He was a man of social and familial concerns. He worked very hard to train his sons and put everything into bringing them up, realising their talents, their idiosyncrasies and inclinations, and let them develop in their own natural way. Pawan was the technocrat, so in the initial stages, he was in charge of all the offset machines, new technologies. Sudhir he knew was the down-to-earth manager, so he gave him that job. Girish was outgoing and enterprising, so when he started DNA, he sent him to Mumbai."

The Bhaskar boys, now the Bhaskar bosses, were aware of their father's ultimate desire and all three joined forces, like fingers clasped together to make a strong fist, to turn it into a tangible reality.

Sudhir who slipped easily into his father's shoes divulged, "There were a few fundamentals my father was very clear about. The first was, come what may, all of you have to stay together united. He would often tell me that whatever happens in life, you must live together happily. One shouldn't slog to death only to earn, one must be happy too while earning. He handed that piece of advice to all 12 of us, our spouses and kids included. So even Pawan's son Kushaan who's the youngest will also tell you, 'Baba used to say that we should all stay together and we should be happy.' Thus, all the kids too have grown up accepting that this is the way we are and this is how we're going to be."

It was achievable because, "Nobody is trying to be somebody else.

"Papa's second point was, everybody knows that this is our strength. So all of us are aware that we are very strong because we are together.

"Third: that we accept each other the way we are. All three of us have a very different character and personality but we understand and celebrate the differences. Each has his own strength. We recognise it and we are able to optimise those strengths.

"Dad's fourth reasoning was that amongst us, there is no power game.

"The fifth, I would say, is that everybody has his own space. But we also have a lot of mutually agreed norms that everybody abides by as a family.

"My children too know that they are not only answerable to us, they are answerable to all three sets of parents. These were the basics that my father insisted on and we have passed them on to our kids. That's how the bonds remain strong in the family."

That was the voice of wisdom, the voice of the eldest in the family.

The youngest brother who also spoke of it, sourced it to his father's style of functioning.

"First and foremost, when we worked together, we were not treated like his sons. In the office, we were four people working together. But once we came home, the hierarchy kicked in. It has been very clear to us right from the beginning that this in the pyramid, this is your older brother, this is the younger. Ever since we were born that respect for hierarchy has been in-built in us. We have maintained it. We don't bring the business into the family and vice versa. That's how we've maintained the balance.

"Our roles are clear," Pawan said but reiterated, "We don't work together because of our roles. We are together because we want to work together. We know that our real strength is in our unity."

Enthused by the togetherness, he revealed, "The energy that we draw from each other comes from being together. In the last 20 years, there have been a few times when we have done things on our own because of certain circumstances, like the others not being able to give much time to some particular aspect. But during those periods we have felt very hollow, very empty. We would have enjoyed it more if we'd done it together."

Pawan didn't even want to think that he was missing his father. "I don't actually," he insisted. "He is still around. I don't ever feel that he's no longer with us.

"I see him around in the form of my brothers," he disclosed his intense personal feeling. "I see him in both Sudhir bhaiya and Girish bhaiya when we're working. He has transferred that energy of his to them and kept himself alive. That's the bond I share with both my brothers."

Pawan also described the work ethic which keeps their feet firmly on terra firma. "We are not sharing a business," he said, "we are serving a business. That's how we look at ourselves. We are serving this organisation. We don't treat it as ours, don't look at it as something we own. We are servants to this organisation.

"We have no *shauq*, no indulgences. We don't do things like taking 50 or 100 days off for a holiday. We're not built like that. At the most we just travel a bit. That too for relaxation to come back refreshed and get back to work. All three of us are like that. Work and family oriented."

'Work' and 'family' were the two key words that drove Ramesh Chandra Agarwal and he passed on the twin chant to his successors.

That's what those who've seen the family function as one inseparable force also state.

"The family is very bonded and they have always been working in joint consultation with each other. The best part is that they all look up to Sudhirji," said Dr Bharat Agarwal. "Even Rameshji used to call him 'Sudhirji'. He would never say, 'Ask Sudhir, or check with Sudhir'. He would always say, 'Ask Sudhirji. Check with Sudhirji'. Sudhirji got that respect from his father from early adulthood.'"

Dr Bharat too foresaw that the problems that beset other business families "won't happen here because they have a very structured way of working. They meet once in a month, a proper family board meeting where all small and big decisions are taken. And all three of them abide by the family board decisions."

If the handing over of the reins was crease-free with consistency prevailing and not fraught with overhaul and upheaval, it was DB's own trusted employees, around to witness two generations at work, who knew best what happened to them after the suddenness of 12 April 2017.

Senior Vice-President Vinay Maheshwari noted, "It was always the way it is today. Sudhirji, Girishji and Pawanji were always the business champs. It's the wisdom, the thought, the icing on the cake, a touch of glow that I'm missing today."

Pradyumna Gopalkrishna Mishra, the Group CFO who knew every amount, however tiny or big, that came in and went out of DB, was of the opinion that the guidance of an expert could never be fulfilled by anyone else. "But," he added, "you cannot wallow in grief, you have a responsibility towards your employees, your company, your stakeholders. All of us are together in trying to fulfil his dream. It's a challenge for us.

"And it's definitely happening—the team is working together under the charge of his three sons. Earlier, the four of them took decisions at family board meetings. Now three of them take it. I'm confident they will take the DB Group to the next level which was Rameshji's aspiration. I'm 101 per cent sure that the three brothers will stay and work together."

Managing Editor Jagdish Sharma said dramatically and emotionally, "As the architect, he built a structure with a strong foundation and strong pillars. The architect has taken care that this structure can withstand any wind, storm or earthquake. I don't see any changes. In this company, even if the owners have worked on something and you have a problem with it, if you can convince them, they'll be fine with it. There's no ego at play."

Chief Technology Officer RD Bhatnagar voiced his reasons for the harmonious working of the brothers. "The Hindi word for it is *sanskaar*," he said. "The *sanskaar* was given to them by both their mother and Chairmansaab for the entire family to stay together. I have noticed that whenever Sudhirji saw Chairmansaab coming towards him, he would bend and touch his father's feet even before thousands of people. Similarly, I saw at the railway station that when Sudhir was alighting from the train, his brothers touched his feet. It's this *sanskaar* that binds them together."

"God has been kind," said Pawan's wife, Nitika who provided a daughter-in-law's view from inside the family. "The three of them won't even move a brick without all of them knowing about it."

Looking at the harmonious family Ramesh Chandra left behind, his nephew, Dr Sunil Garg observed, "One reason I'd think was that my uncle was like the Buddha, not a materialistic person. He believed in relations."

Namita's father, SK Golcha of the grand Golcha Group of Jaipur, saw the Agarwals as perfect brand ambassadors of the joint family tradition. "I cite this DB family as an example to others, to families today where the tallest of them keep fighting. For what? For nothing," he said dismissively.

Admiring the manner in which they functioned as a family, he gave credit first to "Bhabhisa" and then Rameshji. "From the very beginning, they inculcated family harmony in all of them. I know from Girish and Namita that they used to have a family meeting every month where they were all given liberty to say whatever they wanted. Rameshji would say, 'Don't talk behind my back, talk in front of me.' And they would not rise from the meeting until every matter was sorted out. That culture was continued for years and it has been taken over by the next generation. I appreciate Sudhir taking over his responsibility so well. His wife Jyoti also would bother more about Namita-Girish's son Shourya than her own children."

He continued astutely, "In every family, there are discussions and decisions taken, but there has to be one decision maker. That decision maker was Rameshji. Now it's Sudhir."

The next generation grew up more privileged and pampered than its parents but was fortunate to have known a grandfather who forged a special bond with each of them and led them by example.

'One of the most powerful handclasps is that of a new grandbaby around the finger of a grandfather.' Joy Hargrove's beautiful words were experienced by Ramesh Chandra when Shubh, his first grandchild, was born to Jyoti and Sudhir on 25 September 1996.

The perky graduate who studied Business Administration and specialised in Marketing, Operations and Entrepreneurship from Emory University in Atlanta, basked in the attention showered on her as the first-born in a joint family. She happily accepted, "I was born three-and-a-half years after my parents' marriage, and I was everybody's *laadli* (favourite).

"When I was born, Girish Chacha, Pawan Chacha, Bua (Aunt Bhawna), nobody was married. So all their friends were also Chachus and Buas for me. My childhood was spent going *godi se godi*, from one lap to another. I was never a clingy sort of child who wanted only her parents."

Being the eldest in the pecking order, Shubh was the only

grandchild who was close to her grandmother and remembers her with clarity.

"For the longest time, I used to sleep between my grandparents," she cheerfully divulged. "My grandmother passed away when I was about seven-and-a-half years old. She'd tell me all the Bhagwanji stories and teach me religious songs. Grandmothers are loving and emotionally attached to their grandchildren. Earlier, my grandfather was this busy person who was always working, I didn't get close to him. But later, as I grew up, we got talking a lot more."

The hectic travelling by Ramesh Chandra and his sons as they launched various editions in different states found Shubh too on the road. "When I was 40 days old, my father (Sudhir) was launching the Rajasthan edition, so we moved to Jaipur, then to Jodhpur, Chandigarh, Bhopal, Ahmedabad (when my grandmother fell ill), and finally, back to Bhopal."

Shubh was also the first one from this generation, and the first girl in the family, to step out and study abroad. Her grandfather was all for it especially since studying in Bhopal posed a unique problem for her.

"Bhaskar had such a strong presence, the hotel was ours, the mall was ours, the press was ours, we were everywhere with an overwhelming presence. In fact, the first two years at Sanskaar Valley School which my mother started, were very hard because even if I did anything well, I'd never get the credit for it. It would always be, 'Oh, it's your mother's school' or 'It's because you're from Bhaskar.' So my mother decided to send me to Singapore.

"Baba always called me Shubhram," she chirped on. "When I was young, he used to wear only a white safari suit. After years, he started wearing jeans, T-shirt, shorts. I became much closer to him after Dadi passed away."

She was fortunate to be old enough to learn much from Ramesh Chandra.

"The two biggest takeaways from his life were 1) That he was very social. Whether the CEO of a company or a cyclewala, he connected with people at all levels. And 2) He was so humble, he never fussed about anything. When he came to see me in Singapore with Bua and Vivaan, we took him to a Rahat Fateh Ali concert, he was fine with it. We took him for Thai food, he was fine. He enjoyed all of it. When I went to America, he told me, 'I think I should come for your graduation.' I said, 'Of course you have to.' But he passed away one year before I graduated," she said, registering her regret.

"Over the years, all of us kids had become closer to Baba. Even on our annual family holidays, in South Africa, Maldives, Malaysia, everywhere, he'd always enjoy everything, not complain that he had to walk much, or about the food or anything."

But yes, he did not let them cross the line. And on the rare occasion when they did, the benign grandfather was quite capable of giving them a good dressing down.

Shubh disclosed one such incident. "We were in South Africa where a family had called all of us to their house for dinner," she narrated. "We didn't know them but they knew that the Bhaskar family was in town, so they had invited us over. But all of us fussed about it and cribbed, 'Our last two days, why do we have to go there and eat Indian food?' Baba didn't say anything when we were going but after we came back he fired all of us in the lobby. He said, 'When I'm taking all of you with me, you should feel privileged, you should feel blessed.' That was the one time I remember him getting really angry."

Hearing his life story directly from him in Malaysia was also an unforgettable experience. "Without holding back anything, he told us his full story, including the tensions with his father and his humble beginnings. He gave us all the positives and the negatives, so we know what life is all about. There were many things I didn't know like the political problems they faced during the Rajasthan launch.

"I was in always in awe of him and had great respect for him," she stated. "He too was proud of us but would never say it outright. But you knew that deep down he felt proud of you. Like in our old house in Ibrahimpura, I'd started a vocational centre for women, for the underprivileged, the victims of the gas tragedy and so on. This was for girls to learn a craft like tailoring or stitching or a beautician's course to get work later on. He was very happy with it and told me, 'That's a very good thing to do.' But it wasn't like he'd say, 'Wow', and praise you sky high."

For Shubh, some of the most cherished moments she spent with her grandfather were, "Those few days when he came to visit me in Singapore. I always thought there'd be limitations to where you could take him. But he was so open to everything that they turned out to be really memorable for me. He saw my school, my room, met my friends."

On his sudden departure from their lives, she said wisely, "It was a wonderful way for him to go. We are only being greedy when we say he should have lived longer. But for him it was a great way to go."

It was when his grandfather died that Shourya, the eldest male in the new generation, revealed how seriously he took his role.

Shourya himself was weeping inconsolably as he was the grandson closest to Ramesh Chandra. But he brushed aside his tears when he realised that his cousin Arjun would be feeling bereft in Bhopal since the rest of them were still to get there. He called up Arjun and said with grown-up sensitivity, "Don't worry, I'm coming and I'll take care of you."

He was 16, and Arjun 14. But it gave the latter the solace he needed at that moment.

His father Girish was barely 17 and in Class 12 when

he'd started taking care of the Gwalior edition. So the sense of responsibility that Shourya showed at 16 perhaps swam naturally in the Agarwal genes. But a lot more was acquired while growing up with Baba, his grandfather, with many value systems ingrained in him right from birth. One of which was that he would grow up and join the family business.

"Baba always liked to venture into new things and explore new avenues. I also want to do that," said Shourya who enrolled at Northwestern University in Chicago, USA, to study Industrial Engineering in 2018.

The circumstances were vastly different when Ramesh Chandra went adventurously into the family business followed by his sons who too got into it in a climate unfamiliar to the third generation. This was a more privileged set with millennial targets, talking a new language.

"Like all youngsters, I also want to have a successful start-up or something which eventually becomes a big company. I have a list of ideas that I have written down. I know I am privileged and fortunate to have my family support and financial backing," Shourya conceded. "Morally and experience-wise too, they are there for me."

When he saw that his teenage grandson had a head full of questions, Ramesh Chandra steered him gently towards the family business.

"I would ask Baba all my questions about why we don't do this and why we do that because he was the most patient person around," remarked Shourya as tears welled up in his eyes. He wept as he talked of the grandfather who was his lifeline. "It was also very comforting to ask him questions. Papa wouldn't give me straight answers but right from the start, Baba always answered my queries. I could ask him anything and he would explain everything in detail. That's how he got me involved with what was happening in the business. For example, if the family board meeting happened to be in Mumbai, Baba would tell me to take a day off from school and ask me to just come and sit there." It was simply to let Shourya get a feel of what it would be like.

Shourya was also emotionally involved with one nook in his Mumbai house. "I have a very strong memory of this exact place in my house where Baba would be sitting in the morning; he used to go to office only in the afternoon. He would wake up early and sit there reading the newspaper. I would wake up and join him, just sit there for an hour while he read the paper, and then we'd talk.

"I remember when I was 10 years old, he promised me that after three years of living in Mumbai, we'd shift back to Bhopal because I love Bhopal," recalled Shourya.

"So when I was 13, I actually went to him and asked him about it and he was like, *karenge, karenge* (we'll do it). But after that he made it a point to come to Mumbai every month for three days and spend time with us over a weekend. He made sure that we met every month."

Ramesh Chandra's formula of an annual holiday together to further foster togetherness drew Shourya closer to him. Because he was the grandchild who'd move into his Baba's room and take care of him.

Baba was also the family elder who handled his grandson's moods with kid gloves. As Shourya said, "I was very aggressive and stubborn. I was extremely short tempered too after we shifted to Mumbai. I'd get upset and angry very easily. Maybe the change in cities triggered something in me. It was a cultural shift also for me because at that time I didn't even know English, so there were a lot of adjustments to be made. One night, Baba had come down to see us in Mumbai. Normally, whenever I saw him, I would go and touch his feet. But I was so angry that day that when he arrived, I just walked away. Baba didn't say anything but Papa got so angry he pulled me by the ear, dragged me all the way to the room and said, 'Never do that again.' I was eight or nine years old but I will always remember that incident."

In Shourya's aggressive years, Baba was the one with the soothing touch. "When I was in Class 6, and my final exams were around the corner, Baba made me promise him that I would do well and be one of the top 10 in my class. He made me write that on a paper and sign it, then stick it on my pin board. After that I actually started doing well in my studies."

The grandfather's specialty was in crossing generations and communicating in a way that didn't make the child feel he was being patronised.

"And on my part, I really liked taking care of Baba. Whenever we travelled, I used to stay with him in his room. At night, I would massage his feet before he slept. In the morning I used to make tea for him. Whatever he wanted, he would just have to tell me and I would willingly do it for him. I really liked doing things for him and for Nanu, my mother's father."

Teenagers of a college-going age normally like to hang out with their own friends on special occasions. But in the Bhaskar family, festivals, including the rituals associated with them, were celebrated together in Bhopal. One of Ramesh Chandra's achievements was that he succeeded in gathering the younger generation under his roof in a way that they actually looked forward to them without complaining as teenagers are wont to.

"One thing he always stressed on was, *daro nahi, himmat se karo* (never fear, do whatever you have to with courage). Whenever I had an exam or something and I'd call him up, that's what he would always tell me."

By watching him, Shourya also learnt humility.

"For us, he was always just Baba, very humble and down to earth. But if you looked at him from the perspective of the world, he was such a big personality. We never realised it because he didn't have the slightest trace of ego or an air of superiority. We weren't even aware of what he'd achieved, the high position he held in society, until he left us. I realised it after reading about him as a business tycoon. When you click on Madhya Pradesh, his name comes up. He knew so many people. There were tributes from Ministers and Chief Ministers from all over the country, even the Prime Minister. But he never showed off or let you know how important he was. He never went around with a bodyguard or sought attention or want to be in the limelight.

"I need to learn that," Shourya accepted.

A major factor that helped the cousins bond was explained by Shourya who revealed, "I don't call them my cousins—they are my brothers and sisters. Because we are growing up separately, there may be small differences but the good thing is that everybody is very clear and transparent about it. We keep meeting and discussing all this. What also keeps us going is that everybody is very adjusting. I may be less so because I am slightly fussy, a tad picky and short-tempered. But everybody adjusts and adapts to one another's nature.

"Also, we don't have the concept that this is mine and that is yours. Everything is everybody's. Like the Bhopal house belongs to all of us, so does our Mumbai house. There is a spirit of sharing everything which keeps us together, touch wood."

Diva who was 15 years old when Ramesh Chandra passed away, pointed out that although 'Shourya bhaiya' was closest to him, all the grandkids had a special equation with him.

"Because there were things that we always did together," said Namita and Girish's daughter. "Like on Diwali, Baba used to play *maang patta* (an Indian card game) with all of us. My younger brother Kushaan was really small, and he would be really fascinated watching grown-ups play cards on Diwali which we as kids couldn't. So Baba used to play *maang patta* with all of us which is the simplest possible card game."

Aware that Shourya and Diva bickered furiously as siblings normally do, whenever he'd meet them, Ramesh Chandra would ask his granddaughter, 'Has Shourya stopped fighting with you?' "That's something I miss when we go to Bhopal," she said with the simplicity of an unsullied 16-year-old.

Bhopal, of course, spelt home—a recurring refrain with all the kids. "We just love Bhopal so much, any chance we get, we want to go back home. When there's any festival, the first thing you think of is going back home which is Bhopal. Especially for the Diwali celebrations which are so grand. Since we were kids, we didn't play cards with money. So we were really fascinated watching Baba play with all his friends. I remember Vivaan, Kushaan, Arjun and I used to take turns to stand next to him because any time he won, he'd give us a bit of that money."

For Diva, grandfather was the man who never whined about anything.

"Once, when we were all holidaying in Orlando, it was really hot but we kids were really excited to be in Disneyland. So we were running from one ride to the other. Baba patiently waited for us in a restaurant till we finished all our activities for the day. At that time we didn't think it was such a big deal. But looking back, I really appreciate his nature. Even after we got back at the end of each day, it wasn't like he wanted to immediately head back home or anything like that. He was fine. He was happy to just see us having fun and being together."

That togetherness would have seen them all in Bhopal if grandmother Sharda Devi had not passed away so early in life. Even the grandchildren who barely remembered her were aware of the difference her presence would have made.

"My Badi Mummy (Jyoti) tells me that if Dadi had been with us today, she would never have let Papa come to Mumbai and Chachu (Pawan) go to Delhi. When she said that I wished,

'Wow, if only all of us could just go back to living there together again.' But I know it can't happen now," Diva pragmatically accepted.

"When Shourya and I were kids, every time we went to Bhopal for our holidays, we would cry on the flight back. And I remember, we used to make Mamma promise that in one year's time we would all go back to Bhopal. We actually believed that it would happen and were ready to pack up and move there."

Diva repeated what her brother Shourya had said. That there was no word like cousin. "Some things just stay with you," she remarked. "So when we were kids, if I went to my friend's or my friends came over, and I was with Arjun or Kushaan or Shubhdi or any of them, we never introduced them as cousins. As kids, we were always told that 'cousins' is not a word in our dictionary, that we were all brothers and sisters."

And Baba was the 'solution man' for all of them. "If there was any problem in the house, even the smallest one, or if I had to make a decision or was confused about anything, the first person I'd think of was Baba. For us, he was someone who had a solution for everything. I miss him for that. Shourya bhaiya has a very bad temper. Mamma sometimes can't explain stuff to him but Baba could speak to him and he would understand. It's at times like these that I feel we have lost someone so precious."

The day he passed away was, "one I can't ever forget, I remember every minute of it minutely," said Diva, wondering if what she had experienced a day before had been a premonition. "One day before Baba passed away, just out of the blue, I asked my mother, 'Why do we burn people when they die?'" Her mother was baffled that she had harboured such a thought.

Losing him was sad indeed, but the most poignant moment, she said, was watching her grandfather's aged mother weep inconsolably when her son was being taken away for cremation. After that irreparable loss, Diva's great grandmother disconnected from the world, turning to God more than ever before. Religion could sometimes be the great reliever in times of extreme distress. But even if her son, her Hanuman was no more, he had left behind a large and caring family to take on his role, to do everything possible to keep his bereft mother in comfort.

After his passing, the first festival that came around was *Rakhi*—an occasion when Diva really missed her grandfather's presence in the Bhopal house.

"With Shourya and me always fighting, one of our *rakhi* traditions was that he would run away and refuse to have a *rakhi* tied on his wrist by me. Every year, Baba and Papa had to pin him down till I had tied my rakhi on him. But this time, Shourya didn't do anything like that and it was something all of us noticed and missed."

The reminders were many.

"We always have a *Govardhan Puja* (during the Diwali week) where you go around a make-believe mountain and every year, Baba would lead it. He would have a competition with a *laddoo* in a bowl in the middle. Whoever managed to take that *laddoo* was the winner of the game. Everybody was sad and really missed him at the *Govardhan Puja,* after he passed. Bade Papa now leads it."

Diva also treasured the wisdom in the simple, everyday utterances of her grandfather. Like the time the family got Tuffy, their first dog in Bhopal. For the first time in many years, Ramesh Chandra left his ground floor room and went up to where everybody was playing with the new pet in the house. When Jyoti mentioned how expensive a dog was, he had replied, '*Pyaar karne walon ki koi keemat nahi hoti,* there can be no price tag on love.'"

It was simply another message-loaded line from him that found favour with everyone, cutting across generations.

In the special relationship that the grandfather built with

each of his grandchildren, a chord that was unseen to them was that he was actually binding not just him to them but also all of them together. And the takeaways from his life were plenty.

"Till I was seven or eight years old, I was unaware of his achievements," averred Arjun, who is Jyoti and Sudhir's son. "It was actually after he passed away, when I saw the number of people who were talking about him and were affected by his demise, that I realised how he had impacted so many lives."

Born on 28 October 2002, he didn't remember his grandmother at all. But his grandfather was the go-to person for everything. This included the time he was nervous about his final year exams in school. "When I spoke to him about my nervousness, he really motivated me."

One incident which proved a value lesson was when Arjun was playing cricket in the garden with Kushaan.

"Two or three *bhaiyas* (domestic helpers) were watching, helping us, fetching the ball etc. Baba came and whispered to me, 'Just the two of you playing won't be much fun. Why don't you ask the *bhaiyas* to join in and play with you?' That made me realise what a humble man he was. To him it didn't matter where they came from, who they were." It was a big lesson on both humility and inclusion, sensitive traits that Ramesh Chandra made sure he passed on to the third generation.

There were many such qualities that the children absorbed from him. "Once, when one of my report cards wasn't up to the mark," remembered Arjun, "he was absolutely okay with it. He told me, 'You can't expect to do well all the time. It's okay to fail, it's fine if you don't always get what you expected.' I always remember one quote of his: 'Nobody can take away your destiny from you, so don't worry.' He was also someone who was rarely ever stressed. In fact, he would often tell my father at the dinner table, 'Don't worry, *ho jayega*, it'll work out.'

"On the soft boards over our study tables, we have pinned

a sheet with all his words of wisdom related to work, business, and social and family life, on it. His main concern was to keep the family together. It's because of him and what he taught us that we are all very close to each other. Whatever our arguments, he would patiently sort them out."

It made Arjun decide early in life to spend more time with his workaholic father. "I've decided that every Sunday, if my father is in town, I'm going to be with him at home."

Very organically, Arjun looked up to Shourya as the older brother. "Shourya bhaiya is very dedicated to what Baba used to say about family. He believes in it 100 per cent and will never go against it. He's very particular about being with family on particular days and on special occasions.

"In today's world, especially with my generation, it's very rare to spend festive occasions with family and not friends," Arjun agreed. "But I always stay with my family because I know that the largest amount of fun and belonging is with them."

The day he lost Baba was clear in Arjun's mind.

"When I returned home from school around 1.30, I saw all the *bhaiyas* talking. I had a snack as always, but I saw my mother and Maasi (mother's sister), looking very upset, I'd never seen my mother like that. She said to me, 'I want to tell you something.' I stopped eating and asked her, 'What happened?' She said, 'We've lost Baba.' I couldn't understand it at once. Then she hugged me and started crying. I was in a state of shock. I couldn't believe it. Then I went down and saw my mother crying while talking to my father over the phone.

"Papa wasn't home at that time, he came later with Pawan Chachu. Before that day, I had never seen him cry. That's when I broke down. I got a call from Shourya bhaiya around 3.30 in the afternoon. He was worried for me, he said, 'Don't worry, it will be okay. I'm coming there, I'll be there to take care of you, be strong for your parents.'

"At night, when Baba's body was brought home, it was impossible for me to look at it. Everybody was devastated."

In his lifetime, he had worked to keep the family as one. His finale too was with a flourish as Ramesh Chandra did what several patriarchs of business failed to do—he brought the family closer than ever before.

"Two or three days after Baba died, all us siblings sat together and spoke about how to handle it, how to handle our parents," disclosed Arjun. "Shourya bhaiya talked about the *katha,* and how Baba had met everybody there. The day he died, Baba was in Delhi in the morning. He'd seen off Miraya and Kushaan, which he'd never done with any of us. It felt as if he almost knew what was going to happen and he did everything like it was meant to happen. That he didn't suffer, that it happened in a good way, made us accept it better."

With each one finding his own way of coming to terms with it, Arjun began to write to him as if he were still alive.

"In situations where I feel I'm in a fix, I miss him the most," he said. "On my laptop, I keep writing to him, so I don't feel he's not there for me. When we got our second dog, I wrote to him about that. When I was troubled about my exam result, I wrote to him. So that makes me feel he's still there for me."

Miraya and Kushaan, the youngest pair of siblings in the DB family, were the privileged sister and brother who saw their grandfather in Delhi hours before he boarded the Indigo flight to Ahmedabad.

Barely into her teens, Nitika and Pawan's daughter Miraya, like every child in the family, had her own special status in Ramesh Chandra's heart: after all she was born on 8 May 2004, his wedding anniversary, making him believe that Sharda Devi was reborn in the family.

For Miraya, Baba was simply her, "Role model".

Baba, on his part, revelled in the role of grandfather and

would go the extra mile to get to know each of them individually, even learning to play their favourite games.

"He would play Tumbling Monkey and Monopoly with us. He would first understand the game and then play it," she recorded, not quite realising that this simple gesture went beyond making a connection with them. Playing games that the kids liked revealed three of his facets; the eternal child in him, his unquenched curiosity to keep learning something new and his undying but entirely natural instinct to create strong bonds all around him.

"On his last day too, he'd spent the entire day with us in Delhi," she noted. "I took him all around the colony, he didn't once complain that I was making him walk so much."

Memories were like warm, freshly-baked muffins and Miraya had two stand-out ones. One was Baba's fondness for green chutney and *nimbu* (lemon), two constants on any dining table he sat at. "Once," she remembered, "we went to his friend's place, only he and I. They had made *daal baati* (a Marwari specialty) and Baba asked for chutney there too! It was a special outing for me because that was the one time when it was only he and I who went there."

Tuning into his grandchildren's mindspace and being attentive to what they wanted came in different forms. At a Dassera celebration where he was an important part of the function, he saw the kids getting restless as speaker after speaker went up to have his say. There were a few more waiting for their turn at the mike when Ramesh Chandra simply went up and announced, "Now we'll start the ceremony of burning of Ravan," even as the compere desperately tried to tell him that some more speeches remained before Ravan could be burnt.

"He knew that we were bored and that we were only waiting for Ravan's effigy to be set on fire," she said with deep appreciation for his thoughtful intervention.

Born two years after her, Kushaan, the youngest of the six, remembered that he was so close to his grandfather that if he could share anything with his mother, "I could share it with Baba too."

Kushaan also spoke of a workshop-like session his grandfather would conduct with all of them.

"At these sessions where all the cousins met him together and would discuss different things with him, he would ask, 'What do you think is wrong with your brother or your friend?' If there was a problem, he would resolve it. Once I told him, 'If I'm racing, I'm afraid of who's behind and that he will overtake me.' He told me, 'Focus as if you're racing all alone'.

"All that he told me helped me a lot. Talking to him like this wasn't a formal thing, we were very comfortable with him. He was so approachable, we could even wake him up to play with us. Sometimes even in the rain, he'd play football with us."

"All of us along with my father, wrote down all that we had learnt from him. Each of us has a copy of it pasted on the wall at the study table. Shourya bhaiyya made that for us," he added.

'Grandchildren are the dots that connect the lines
from generation to generation – Lois Wyse

The connection with his grandfather thus continued with what was up on the wall. "If there's any competition, we read through that. And we pray to him in the mandir before going to school. When I enter the mandir I feel very nice, I just forget all my worries," said Kushaan, suddenly the little boy again.

'I want to leave a legacy,
How will they remember me?
Did I choose to love?
Did I point to you enough?'

Sang Nichole Nordman.

Ramesh Chandra Agarwal could tick off all the above boxes and more.

The name Kushaan, the youngest inheritor of Generation Three, translates into 'Dynasty'. Very apt when applied to a legacy that smoothly blends Bhaskar & Sons with Bhaskar & Grandsons.

Chapter 7

THE FAMILY FAREWELL

'Say not in grief that they are gone,
but give thanks that they were yours'

—Hebrew Proverb

On Sunday, the weekend after Morari Bapu's *katha* had revitalised the family and left Ramesh Chandra exhilarated like he'd scaled Mount Everest, Jyoti asked him, "Papa, would you like to go out for a South Indian dinner tonight?" He who was always game with a willing, '*Chalo*, let's go' to every suggestion from his children, togged up in jeans and a red tee and turned it into an impromptu foursome date with his mother, Sudhir and Jyoti.

On Wednesday, 12 April 2017, when Man Friday Hemant dialled her number in distress, Jyoti was at a meeting at Sanskaar Valley School. Frenzied phone calls began to be exchanged between Jyoti and Dr Bharat Agarwal, Jyoti and Girish, Jyoti and Sudhir.

"We hadn't really understood the gravity of the situation at that time but I felt something was terribly wrong, so I called up Girish," she looked back. "I told him to rush to Ahmedabad. Bharat has told me Papa has had a cardiac arrest. I said, 'Do something, Hemant has told me they're trying to resuscitate his heart.'"

Before Jyoti could reach the airport to go to Ahmedabad, she got the shattering news that the irrevocable had happened, news that the golden hour had come and gone, and there was nothing anybody could do anymore.

Sudhir was out of town, Girish and Namita were in Mumbai, and Pawan and Nitika, the two family members to have met him last, just a few hours earlier, were in Delhi.

Nitika, the last family member to bid him farewell, retraced his steps before he took that final one on the escalator in Ahmedabad.

"In fact, he had his last breakfast with me before he left for Ahmedabad," came her flash from the past. "He was completely hale and hearty. He had some fruit and coconut water, then he left for Ahmedabad... never to come back."

When he had a meeting lined up in Ahmedabad, why he took the circuitous route from Bhopal via Delhi was because of a phone call that Nitika had made to him on 8 April.

"After the *katha*, he was at the peak of his happiness—he had met everybody in good spirits and had spent quality time with them. When we returned to Delhi after the *katha*, I had called him up to say that Kushaan wasn't settling down well and was getting anxious about school. I asked him to please come down to Delhi and talk to Kushaan. He called me back in 15 minutes and said, 'I'll be there on the 11th.' He had cancelled everything to come here."

He reached Delhi in the morning, Pawan was away, the kids were in school. So he spent the whole morning with Nitika. "The kids came home at 4 pm. So until then, we had lunch, we talked the normal father-daughter stuff and we watched TV. I told him that he must come and stay with us for at least 10 days. After his afternoon nap, we took a walk around the neighbourhood in the evening to show him our new house that was getting ready. I even showed him his room. He had kept undivided time for us. And Kushaan slept with him that night.

"Next morning, he had a half-hour meeting with Pawan who was travelling and had just got back. He also saw the kids off when they left to catch the school bus. He hugged Kushaan, told him not to be anxious about anything, to call and speak to him and that he'd come and see him again. When he left for the airport at 7.30 am, he was in the pink of health, there was no pain, no sign of breathlessness or discomfort. Nothing was amiss, he was absolutely fine. The guard at the service apartment remembered that Papa had patted him and asked him where he was from. Imagine, just a random guard standing outside the service apartment. The guard later told me, 'Bhabhi, people don't usually talk to us so nicely.' And for him, Papa was really someone very important. But that was the kind of man he was—reaching out and touching people's hearts in different ways."

Three hours later, he had stepped onto that escalator.

"We don't feel he has gone away," she remarked. "We feel he is still with us. I always say, 'This is Papa's room.' We've done it up as his room."

In Bhopal, Meena Garg, still dazed at what she'd heard about her brother, hurried across to join Jyoti. Children, grandchildren, everybody was catching a flight from somewhere to reach Bhopal. Girish and Namita flew from Mumbai to Ahmedabad to escort the embalmed mortal remains of Ramesh Chandra to his hometown from where he'd begun his incredible journey of profit and philanthropy.

The most delicate and heartbreaking part of his abrupt

departure was the moment when news of the unfortunate happening had to be tactfully conveyed to Taiji, Ramesh Chandra's aged mother, who looked forward to his return, as always. "There were waves of people coming into the house, I knew Papa was not going to be brought home before 7 in the evening," Jyoti revealed. "So we kept Taiji in her room till 5 pm. We reasoned that there was no point getting her all anxious and emotional right through the day. So we let her go about her daily routine."

As late as 5.30, Meena and Jyoti took the brave step of going into her room. Jyoti's father was ailing those days. So when they went in and said, 'Papaji', she thought it was Jyoti's father they were talking about and she sympathised with her saying, 'He was so unwell.' Jyoti then took out her father-in-law's photo and showed it to her to make her understand what had happened. *Putra shok*, the sorrow of losing your child in your lifetime, is said to be the saddest event in a parent's life. Kasturi Devi was inconsolable.

Over the months, her puja routine continued. "She used to talk a lot earlier, but after Papa's passing, she has quietened down," observed Jyoti.

The world watched as the three couples he left behind carried on his prodigious work, never allowing his absence to affect either the work, the family or the society he so cared for. When his first death anniversary came along, they got a special pat on the back from Ramesh Chandra's sister, their aunt Meena. Dispensing with the old custom of feeding brahmins, they made the collective decision to serve a hearty meal to hundreds of children and the underprivileged. "All of them personally served everybody, making sure they were feeding each and every person gathered there," remarked Meena.

"It is very difficult to step into his shoes," said Sudhir frankly, although what society observed of him was that he had slipped into the role with natural grace. "My father was a very different person and he had a few sterling qualities where I don't score well," he said, analysing the areas where he stood apart from his father. "He was a huge risk taker, I am not. I'm cautious in comparison. He was also fearless, I still haven't got there."

Sudhir also conceded, "My father was superbly connected socially which is absolutely contrary to my personality. I don't go out and meet anybody. I don't even go to DB's own functions. He knew that I was far more reserved than he was. Initially, he would say, 'This is not right, you must start meeting people, must network.' But he gradually accepted that this was who I was and would shrug, 'It's your nature, we can't do anything about it.'"

The one outstanding trait Sudhir fondly remembered about his father was, "His humility. He was the humblest man I ever knew."

Namita had her own reservoir of fond moments and memories.

"I clearly remember, it was on 31 January 2016 that all of us were sitting on the terrace in the Bhopal house when Girish and Sudhir bhaiya mentioned to Papa that they would have to shift Pawan to Delhi to take care of the digital wing. For a moment, he was taken aback, 'Why can't you make systems where he can work from here?' He didn't want Pawan to shift because he wanted the family to be together. But once it was explained to him that to make the business grow, it couldn't be done from Bhopal, he came around and said, 'Okay, for the business we'll have to do that, but make sure all of you stay together as a family. Make more systems so that the bond is not lost because at the end of it, family is important.'"

Meena, Ramesh Chandra's younger sister, was the only one before whom their mother Kasturi Devi could bare her heart. When she would drop in for a 4 pm cup of tea with her mother, the elderly lady would hold her hand and shed the tears that she held back from the rest of the family.

Daughter Bhawna who spoke to her father every single day of his life, couldn't speak about him without her eyes welling up.

"He used to play UNO with my son Vivaan and my son would always win," she said, memories flowing along with her tears. "The last time around, Papa was leaving for Indore, but I forced him to stay back and play one game with Vivaan and Papa won that game for a change. He told Vivaan, 'See, I'm not going to lose every time. Nanu has learnt the game now.'" It was a classic Ramesh Chandra moment: the eternal learner mastering even a child's game and making his connection with a generation more than six decades younger to him.

When Bhawna went to Bhopal for the *katha,* she ordered a batch of special diabetic *sandesh* (a Bengali sweetmeat) from Kolkata for her father. "He never ever asked for anything but he liked it so much that he wanted Vishal to get that *sandesh* again when he joined me in Bhopal."

Bhawna continued her reverie.

"In our house in Bhopal we were eight of us but there was always food cooked for at least 12. Somebody or the other would always drop in and join us for a meal. The doors of this house were always open, I don't ever remember them being closed. And Papa loved this, he loved meeting people.

"It's still difficult to accept that he is not with us anymore," she said, teary-eyed. "There have been times when I have called up saying, 'Put Papa on the line.' Papa didn't carry a mobile for the last three or four years of his life. So one was used to telling Hemant or whoever was with him, 'Put him on the line.'"

The last thing that Ramesh Chandra did in his life was to listen to music on his iPod on the flight from Delhi to Ahmedabad. It was the iPod Bhawna had gifted him with all his favourite songs downloaded on it.

"Normally he would sleep on the flight but that day he listened to the music I had given him on the iPod," she said with melancholy and a strange sense of comfort that he had made one last connection with her.

Her husband Vishal watched on and commented, "His death was a total shock. We used to tease him that he looked much younger than his real age, he was so fine and fit and hearty. He still had more hair on his head than all his sons put together."

'Unable are the loved to die, for love is immortality,' said Emily Dickenson. But the family could move from grief to gracious acceptance with able assistance from Philosophy.

Pandit Vijayshankar Mehta from Ujjain eased the pain somewhat for all of them when he humanised Death in the context of Ramesh Chandra: He was such an affectionately simple man that anytime he was asked to come for a drive, to a movie or out for dinner, or anywhere at all, he would smile and say, '*Chalo,* let's go.' So when Ramesh Chandra put his foot on that last step of the escalator, Death offered him its hand and said, 'Shall we go, Ramesh?'

And he said, '*Chalo,* let's go.'

Chapter 8

THE SOCIAL NETWORK

'Success brings to the fore what is inherently within you'

— ANON

It could be either hubris or humility.

What success coaxed out of Ramesh Chandra Agarwal could best be seen when the sitting Chief Minister of a state quoted poet Saqib Lakhnavi and penned a requiem in grief, when a grandchild wept while talking about him more than 18 months later, a grown-up adult, a partner in the textile business sobbed unabashedly in a five-star coffee shop and an employee almost had a nervous breakdown.

The number of men of substance whose eyes turned moist when they talked about him—gender, age and social standing, irrespective—painted the portrait of a man whose abrupt death jolted and created a permanent vacuum in a wide spectrum of friends, family, employees, politicians, bureaucrats and society at large. Emerging through those emotions was a complete picture of Ramesh Chandra Agarwal, lighting up different aspects of his personality—personal, professional and social.

It matters not how many people you're surrounded with in your life, what matters is how many weep when you die.

They were too many to count.

'Bade shauq se sun raha tha zamana
Tum hi so gaye dastan kehte kehte'

(The world sat up, listening spellbound. But you slipped away midway while narrating your saga)

Dr Shivraj Singh Chouhan, three-time Chief Minister of Madhya Pradesh who held the post when Ramesh Chandra died, quoted Lakhnavi and noted poignantly, "He was like my older brother, he gave me a lot of affection. He gave Madhya Pradesh a new identity. He used to go out of his way to help the needy very quietly, not telling his own family about it. That was his nature."

It was Shivraj Singh who emphasised Ramesh Chandra's role in the elevation of Madhya Pradesh as a state. It went far beyond family, DB and certainly, much more than just the bottom-line.

"Through *Bhopal Utsav*, he worked towards giving Bhopal an identity," said Shivraj Singh. "He would work towards bringing different communities together, especially through the Holi and Eid gatherings that he organised every year. He brought society together and set a fine example of secular harmony.

"He brought out the best in people. He worked for various causes like batting for dry Holi to save water. He also championed the cause of not burning trees during Holi to save trees and to save water. He promoted the planting of trees for more *hariyali* (greenery) and was concerned about the environment. He wanted to save the earth for future generations.

"He was the kind of social worker who always thought of

ways of bringing more and more people together, organising programmes, working to bring about understanding, *bhaichara* and love between people."

The point that should draw admiration is that it wasn't a celebrity politician that Ramesh Chandra had impressed. Shivraj Singh knew him from the time, "I was a nobody. I was a *karyakarta* (party worker) and would go on my cycle to distribute news to newspaper offices. He used to think of me as a good worker and encouraged me to keep working harder. He was nice to me from the time I started my political career. The friendship remained the same over the years and I would often seek his advice on various matters, especially those related to investments (*nivesh*) and government spending."

Ramesh Chandra, he said, "worked like the Brand Ambassador of MP," and helped give the state a wonderfully positive image.

"When I had organised the 1st Global Investor Summit in Indore, no industrial house wanted to participate in it. Some people even made fun of this event. In those troubled times, Rameshji not only encouraged me but also supported me wholeheartedly. It was because of his suggestions and his personal equations that well-known industrial houses not only from India but abroad too, participated in the Summit. Because of his efforts, many industrialists invested too in MP."

He added, "Besides being very approachable and accessible, he was in constant, ongoing dialogue with one and all, the real estate sector, soya bean sector, textiles, chambers of commerce and the Vaish (business) community. *Vyapar jagat ke pratinidhi thay,* he also represented the business community and would often come to me with people to discuss their problems."

What also won his unstinted appreciation was Ramesh Chandra's distinctive ability to look at an issue from all sides and be an effective bridge between the people and the government. "He understood the limitations of the government and would tell the people he came with to also keep the good of the government in mind. I liked this quality in him a lot.

"When he would come with the Chambers of Commerce or any business organisation, he would tell them, 'Don't just ask for tax-exemption and rebates because the government also needs revenue, needs to collect taxes to run the state.' Otherwise, associations would come only asking for exemptions.

"Likewise, as a newspaperman too, he was ethical and discouraged irresponsible news being published," noted the former CM. "So his being a newspaperman never affected our friendship. He was not inclined towards any political party. He was friendly with everybody."

A great believer in social networking, Ramesh Chandra's people-skill created deep attachments, however brief the interaction with him.

One of India's leading industrialists, Kumar Mangalam Birla, Chairman of the Aditya Birla Group, labelled the quality time he spent with Ramesh Chandra as memorable and meaningful.

"I had the occasion of meeting Ramesh Chandraji only once but that meeting left a lasting impression on me. The Agarwal family runs a school in Bhopal by the name of Sanskaar Valley School. They had invited me to be the Chief Guest on Founders' Day at the school in 2016.

"Here was a man who was self-made, extremely successful, yet equally down to earth and humane. He was the kind of person one wanted to spend time with and to learn from. At the event, his inaugural address had a moving impact on the audience. There was a palpable sense of the connect that he had with the parents of the students from the school. I came away feeling privileged to have met a man with a vision, a big heart and a dream for India."

Rakesh Jhunjhunwala, a big name on the Bombay Stock Exchange who had no professional association with Ramesh Chandra, looked continuously at four monitor screens before him that scrolled up and down with the greens and reds of the stock market, and at another on the side that updated him on what was galloping at the races where too he was a major player. Pointing to the chairs and sofas behind him, he said that the DB Chairman would drop in once in a while for a friendly chat.

"I met him around 2002-3 and we'd meet three to four times a year. There was never any agenda and we didn't have a business relationship. We had no common business at all."

When DB went public, "I was involved in the advice I gave him but not involved in carrying it out or investing in it.

"Undoubtedly sharp, he actually acted on some of the things I told him," Jhunjhunwala commented and smiled, "It wasn't interaction for the sake of interaction."

The visual he remembered was that of a successful man, "who had a ready smile and a soothing personality. He was always wanting to learn something new. He would discuss a lot of politics and had a very good idea of what was happening around."

Jhunjhunwala was right for Ramesh Chandra always had his ear to the ground.

"Once a month or every two months he would hold meetings going right down to correspondents and the juniormost staff on the marketing side," revealed close friend and bureaucrat Sunil Arora. "I'm told those meetings were very exhaustive. He would often surprise them with his grasp and knowledge of local issues. Any person at the level of Rameshji would have his own means of acquiring information as he would have his own outside sources of inputs.

"His main strength was an innate simplicity and his thoroughness. He wasn't an MBA from an Ivy League but he was thorough. Simple, not simple-minded or simplistic," he shrewdly differentiated between the traits.

Ramesh Chandra liked people. He was a people-person. And

many a professional acquaintance transformed into becoming a lifelong family friend. Sunil Arora was one of them.

"We'd normally meet for lunch at my house. He was very observant, had very telling comments to make on the political developments in Rajasthan, on the ruling party and on the opposition. He was very well informed about Delhi and had a wide range of contacts. The good thing was, he never showed off or dropped names," recalled Sunil.

"Year after year he was on the *India Today* Power List. I have seen people less eminent than him but 10 times more arrogant. He was one of those who took it easy," Sunil Arora said about the friend he'd lost.

That intense feeling of the loss of a family member was heard again and again from a boundless gathering of men, successful, substantial figures in their own field.

One of them was Vivek Agarwal, the Principal Secretary to the CM of MP, a distinguished civil servant. What he said, further polished the picture of Ramesh Chandra, adding dimensions unstated so far to the personality of the late Chairman of DB.

"He was a kind of mentor for me," Vivek acknowledged with a great degree of frankness. "It's interesting how we met. After the Kumbh Mela in 2004, when I was the Collector of Ujjain, the top part of the Mahakaal temple was golden but the small *shikhars* around the main door were plain. There were about 120 of them and we were looking for donors to have them goldplated. I thought the best way would be to meet someone who'd understand it. Rameshji had come to Ujjain for a *darshan*, so I went to meet him and spent about an hour with him. He immediately agreed to take care of 21 *shikhars* and also underwrote the rest saying, 'After you meet other donors, if there are any left to be taken care of, I'll take them.'"

What made the Collector go meet a visitor to Ujjain was because, "I'd heard about him as an industrialist and philanthropist."

That was the beginning of a friendship where Ramesh Chandra's natural skill at making it grow came to the fore.

"Throughout his life, we had conversations. I would get a phone call from him every 15 days just to stay in touch and once a month he would say, 'Let's meet up.' His usual line was, '*Aur naya kya hai* (What's new)?' He was always looking for something new.

"Once, he saw the Indore city bus service, something new that I had introduced. He was staying at Fortune Landmark. He called me and said, 'These buses are beautiful, we should also look at introducing them in Bhopal.' So he called Sudhirji and they actually bought a similar bus for their school Sanskaar Valley. He was always fascinated with new ideas."

Being a sharp, incisive person himself, Vivek was able to peer into matters at DB and put forth his views on Ramesh Chandra Agarwal, the media tycoon.

"Wherever you need money and you need to generate resources to make it self-sustaining, you need a business brain behind it. But of course, how good that business mind is in allowing editorial freedom to professionals, makes all the difference. My take on this family, especially with Rameshji and Sudhirji heading it, is that they don't interfere in the editorial work at all. DB has a cadre of journalists with a system where editors are routinely transferred. No editor stays in one place for more than three to four years but all of them have a long-term association with the group. They have proper compensation packages and job security but they don't allow them to become complacent. DB has a separate team for marketing, editorial people don't go out seeking advertisements. It's purely professionally managed."

Ramesh Chandra was of course much more than a newspaper man, a man on an eternal search for new avenues to step into and explore.

"Once, when I was MD of the Mandi Board and Warehousing Corporation, I was setting up logistics parks and he developed an interest in investing in it. He already had investments in soya bean and soya bean processing but he spent a lot of time with me on it. Though he didn't finally invest in it, his insights on business helped me prepare a proper project and now it's one of the best logistics parks in Central India.

"He would never hesitate to donate money for a social cause and it was never with an ulterior motive.

"His demise was a personal loss for me," he said. "I was there during the cremation but I didn't have the heart to go back and see his picture with a garland. So to this day, I haven't been to his house after that."

More qualities that made the man were provided by OP Rawat, yet another senior bureaucrat.

Once, just once, Ramesh Chandra had tried to enrol the bureaucrat too into his business.

"When he was starting out in Rajasthan, I was in Defence. I once happened to travel with him and his wife from Bhopal to Jaipur. I was going for a meeting and he was going to set up the Jaipur edition. That time he asked me, 'You people work so hard but you don't get returns commensurate with that. So, why don't you just leave and come over to this side?' I said, 'We're not made for it. After spending 20 years or more in this service, we can't really do that.' His wife also intervened and told him, 'He's absolutely right. Right from the start you've been like this, started selling salt, started this and that. Let him be.'"

Rawat also knew Ramesh Chandra closely as a newspaper man. "During the Babri Masjid incident, there were riots in Bhopal and I was Commissioner in the Public Relations Department, MP. I found that one or two big names among the newspapers were doing fictitious stories like a Muslim girl being raped and her body found in a *nullah* (gutter). I realised that with Rameshji at the top, DB wasn't indulging in such scurrilous reporting. I was Commissioner PR for four years but at every turn, I found that he stood out different from the others. His sense of ethics was different."

IAS officer Pradip Baijal from the MP cadre was also clinical in his appraisal of a man he respected and admired. It was sourced to a few incidents that added a few more features to the portrait of Ramesh Chandra.

"He decided to come into the power sector and got a couple of power plants," Baijal noted. "I used to be Joint Secretary Power, I was in that sector (in different positions) for a few years and that's when Mr Agarwal would come and see me. I found his knowledge of the power sector enormous."

It was when Baijal was embroiled in the 2G case that he was able to single out Ramesh Chandra as different from the pack of newspapermen.

"I got into a lot of trouble because of a totally false case filed against me to save the DMK in the 2G case," Baijal stated. "Lots of newspapers who were friends of mine gave me up. Every other day, there would be the news that Baijal is likely to be arrested." But Ramesh Chandra neither distanced himself from Baijal in that controversial hour nor sought headlines from him. He simply kept in touch. "My respect for him went up," explained Baijal.

Another memory dated back to the 1970s. "I was District Magistrate of Bastar for about four years (1973-75). At that time Bastar had seven districts. Later, when I was the Industries Secretary in MP, I thought, we have the richest iron ore in the world but not a single steel plant."

So Baijal made every effort to have a steel plant set up in MP which interested and impressed Ramesh Chandra.

"Two years ago (2016, a year before Ramesh Chandra passed away), Mr Agarwal had an Industrialisation Meeting for MP in

Jabalpur to which he called me as the keynote speaker. He had a full house with the Industries Minister (State), other MPs and Ministers all being there. One of the topics was 'Key Lessons From The Bastar Steel Plant.'"

Baijal asked his host why he had chosen him as a speaker. "I told him, 'I'm not a politician, I was just doing my job.' I felt sorry that the richest primary product in the world was going to China, Japan, Vishakapatnam. They were setting up steel plants all over the world while this poor place was not getting anything. Why? It was the politics of a backward area, of tribal agitation.

"I was surprised that Mr Agarwal recognised this when he went to Bastar. He told me, 'You explain the case to people at the seminar'." Incidents like this set Ramesh Chandra as a man who understood another man's worth. A case of respect begets respect.

Professionally, "I would rate him as an outstanding entrepreneur. He was a big opinion maker," remarked Baijal. "I would tell other people, 'What a man. All you other newspaper men *bewakoof ho uske saamne* (you are nincompoops before him).'"

Baijal underscored the most important element that made Ramesh Chandra Agarwal such an important man in the landscape of North India: "Very few people know that in India it is the Hindi newspapers that rule the country, not the English ones."

If Pradip Baijal was able to astutely assess Ramesh Chandra from an objective distance, another top-level bureaucrat added intimate strokes to his portrait as a friend who knew him both professionally and socially.

Retired Chief Information Commissioner Satyanand Mishra could also trace the growth of DB and the increasing importance of its Chairman from first-hand knowledge of the business.

"I first met Mr Agarwal in 1985 when I was Special Secretary to Chief Minister Motilal Vora. The CM was also dealing with the PR Dept and had a lot to do with newspapers and publications coming from Bhopal. *Bhaskar* was one of the papers which had multiple editions in MP. So Mr Agarwal would visit the Secretariat in that connection once in a while.

"In the modern sense, he was not a very educated person, was not articulate in English nor could he speak at length on any issue. But he had a very keen sense of the goings-on in politics. I think that's the reason many CMs and political leaders belonging to the Congress and the BJP always consulted him. Over the years, his social standing and esteem grew as his media house got bigger. But I don't recall this growth in DB making any great change in his basic nature. He was generally a person who was extremely polite.

"He never made enemies," Mishra pointed out. "If there was any misunderstanding, he would see to it that it was ironed out. One cannot grow if one makes many enemies. He was a self-made man. The newspaper he inherited from his father was nothing. It was he who took it to such heights.

"For those of us who have seen *Bhaskar*, Mr Agarwal and his family growing, it's been amazing because you normally only read about such people. MP is not a place with too many big businessmen. He was one of the first Madhya Pradeshis to become one of the top businessmen of the country."

With Mishra interested in culture as well as PR, he noticed that Ramesh Chandra had, "another side to him that surfaced quite early. He was widely interested in cultural and socio-religious activities, and was associated with several Hindu cultural programmes. If an important religious person was coming to Bhopal and there was a programme, he would be associated with it.

"There is a cancer hospital in Bhopal, the only one in MP called the Nehru Cancer Hospital. He was involved with its management and by the time he passed away, he was probably the Chairman of that trust."

An ardent devotee of Mata Amritanandamayi (Amma) of Kerala, Mishra had invited her to Bhopal in 2004. "By then Uma Bharti had become CM of MP, Digvijaya Singh had just left. It was a very large function that we had for Amma and to organise one on that scale was beyond the capacity of any single individual. Besides his personal contribution, Mr Agarwal also personally chaired many meetings to ensure that the arrangements were in order. Amma visited his house when she came to Bhopal.

"Unfortunately," the brainy bureaucrat remarked, "English newspapers think they are the opinion makers of the country. Some with only a fraction of the circulation of DB are considered important media houses. If there is any English newspaper that's comparable to DB in its reach or depth of penetration, it's only the *The Times of India.*"

Dr RS Goswami, President of the Federation of Chamber of Commerce, commented on another sterling quality of Ramesh Chandra's. "When 95 per cent of the members would find hurdles in government procedures, he would say, 'Look at hurdles as opportunities. These hurdles are what keep the competition, the multi-nationals away. If these hurdles weren't there, the multi-nationals would have wiped you out," he said

Subhash Chandra of Zee TV recalled with fondness, "I met Rameshji when I was President of Agarwal Vikas Trust, an institution in Agroha from where the Vaish community emerged. As President I had toured all the states, *brahman kiya*, and met many people connected with the association. In MP, I met Rameshji who was also at the forefront of these activities. From then on, the mutual affection grew and we became good family friends.

"Once we got closer, we started sharing each other's *sukh-dukh, paarivaarik baatein* (family issues both happy and those that caused concern). If he heard something negative about me, or if he came to know about some government move that would affect me, he would pick up the phone and inform me about it.

"An outstanding quality that I saw in him was that even in an adverse situation, he stood courageous. He had a positive, 'Let's wait and see and keep moving forward' approach. When he notched up very huge losses in the solvent business and I asked him if he needed any help, he said, 'No, no, *theek ho jayega,* it will be resolved.'"

DB, under him and after, stayed apolitical, borne out by the fact that if dyed-in-the-wool RSS worker and BJP leader Shivraj Singh Chouhan mourned his loss, so did Congress *netas* Digvijaya Singh and Kamal Nath who belonged to opposing factions within the same party.

"In the 1990s, he would come to Delhi and we'd meet for lunch. We had become good friends by then," Kamal Nath said, taking time off from the throes of pre-election prepping in Madhya Pradesh, the same elections that catapulted him to the CM's chair in December 2018. "We would go to Lodhi Hotel where they had a South Indian restaurant and enjoy the food there."

The oft-asked question of whether a true friendship was possible between a politician and a media baron was answered by Kamal Nath who observed, "There can be friendship with a newspaperman when you have the understanding that at the end of the day the newspaper cannot be your mouthpiece. On the other hand, it cannot be somebody else's mouthpiece either."

That was the foundation on which this friendship stood.

Kamal Nath remarked, "We became family friends, I have very good relations with his whole family, his sons. Then he branched off into education, power, digital, a lot of other things which was the right thing to do."

It was the same kind of friendship that was struck between

Ramesh Chandra and Digvijaya Singh, another Congress leader. "Ours was the relationship of family friends rather than that of a journalist and a politician," said Singh. "I also received the *baraat* at his daughter's wedding. He had a responsibility to run his paper, I had my job to do as a politician. There was no acrimony over it."

Digvijaya had watched DB climb rung by rung to reach the top.

"DB is the largest circulated daily in MP. Very powerful. It gave respectability to Hindi journalism.

"A newspaper owner meets a wide cross-section of people. Naturally he gets information from all sides, so there used to be more *gupshup*, casual chatting than anything else when we'd meet. Both of us enjoyed that," he wound up crisply.

Ramesh Chandra had three biological sons.

He also treated some others as his fourth.

It would be difficult to discern who this fourth son was.

Was it Dr Bharat Agarwal who was inducted into the family like a fourth son? Or the two young, immensely successful men in Mumbai who both connected with him like a son would?

The Fourth Son Syndrome was a unique singularity in Ramesh Chandra Agarwal.

His relationship with Madhu Kela and Amith Agarwal, exemplified how like-mindedness and rooted simplicity had a tendency to gravitate towards each other in an exchange of admiration. It was reflected in Ramesh Chandra's fondness for stock market maven Madhu Kela and dynamic StarAgri director Amith Agarwal, men younger than him, not bound by blood but bonded by qualities that all of them shared.

The very affable Madhu Kela mirrored much of Ramesh Chandra's traits that included retaining an innate niceness despite immeasurable success; a success that was self-earned through a combination of brainwork and the willingness to both slog and gamble.

"I had a long association with him from 2001 onwards," said Kela. "I got to know him as a curious person, enthusiastic to know and to learn more. He was such a sharp business man. I explained to him the intricacies of the stock market and fortunately made him buy some shares where he made a profit of a few crore rupees. It enabled him to understand that I had the depth and the knowledge of the economy, currency and so on.

"Since I was heading Reliance Mutual Funds at that time, I had all kinds of inputs coming to me and insights into the stock market. Despite the age difference, he developed great fondness for me and I developed great respect for him. A person of his stature who could call up and speak to the Prime Minister but was still so grounded that he could communicate with anybody, was truly unique.

"When they wanted to take DB public, they wanted to understand how to go about it, what to price it at, etc. Then they wanted to go into the power sector, so we discussed that too.

"On 80 per cent of his visits to Mumbai, he would meet me for sure. He would either call me home or we would go out somewhere for a drink. We had a fantastic relationship. We clicked at the very first meeting.

"I would like to say that he had a good commercial acumen and an ability to comprehend a lot of things. He was sharp, he knew what was feasible, and he was very hardworking. We would discuss a lot of subjects, he would ask for my viewpoints on what was happening in India, what was happening in textiles, in currency, and so on. For me talking about him is very emotional, he was more like a father than a friend.

"When I built a new house in Walkeshwar, I was very certain that he would be extremely happy and proud to see what I was able to build," he added with the simple pride of a man who'd done it on his own steam. "I took him to my puja room and I touched his feet saying, 'I know that you're one person who will always wish me good and I need these blessings coming from your heart'. He was so happy for me, he must've told 20 people, *Madhubhai ne kya ghar banaya,* what a house he has built.

"He was fond of having wine in select company. So on his birthday, we had a fantastic time at his place, a gathering of very close friends, with music and singing. He would sometimes call me and say, '*Chalo,* let's go have some wine,' sometimes at the Oberoi, sometimes Taj, wherever. We would talk for two to three hours but it would seem like only 15 minutes had passed by. Time would fly in his company.

"He would sometimes ask me, 'Madhubhai, you have never asked me for anything.' I would tell him, 'You're my insurance policy, my back-up. If I ever need anything, I'll come to you. Though I work for Anil Ambani, you're the person I'll call. And I know that the day I call, you will stand by me.' But no, I never had to cash that 'insurance policy'," he added with a wide smile.

The idea of DB going public in 2009 could be traced to Madhu Kela.

"Initially it was started by me," he acknowledged, "they didn't know the stock market. But the kind of person he was, he quickly picked up enough knowledge about it.

"When I met him, I knew he was undisputedly one of the most influential men in the country. He had access to Sonia Gandhi or Narendra Modi, any person at any level. To have a connect with me, that too such an in-depth one, makes me realise that his success was because of his relationships.

"For a person who was running a successful newspaper business, he was eager to expand and go into many other areas as well. Without being a technical person—he was not an engineer or technician—he went into real estate, power plant, solvent, textiles. He found the right people and put them in the right business. Like he found me to discuss matters of the financial world. And he made people feel comfortable in his company."

Madhu missed those meetings, those conversations, that warmth. "I miss him as my father," he said. "Not as my godfather but as a father," he underlined.

'How are you going to have a dream come true if you don't have a dream in the first place?' What held true for Ramesh Chandra applied to young entrepreneur Amith Agarwal and his three friends who came together with an ambition. Unrelated by blood to each other or to the DB family, it was the agri business that put them in Ramesh Chandra's line of vision.

"We started StarAgri in 2007. Mr Agarwal had a huge agri business, he was the second largest soya processor in MP and we wanted to connect with him and his group, offer them all our services," Amith Agarwal stated frankly. "We started chasing them in 2008 and succeeded in meeting Mr Agarwal in 2009.

"One day he invited us to Jaipur for a meeting where he met us at Rambagh Palace. At that meeting, he said he wanted to do big things in agri, wanted to put up a big processing plant in Kota. He said, 'I see big things happening in the agri sector and I want to be a part of it, I want to double my capacity.' We had a half-day session with him. Agri was very close to his heart from a soul perspective," Amith disclosed. "He would talk of farmer prosperity, how we can give a better price to farmers, better the whole eco system. He would talk about wanting to produce good products from the consumer's point of view too. He would say, 'We should resolve farmers' problems and take care of consumers.' He had that vision. He also started a rice mill.

"One day, he talked about our business plan for StarAgri and asked us in the most straightforward way possible, 'What do you want to become? It's the next phase of your life. Tell me your dreams.' I was clear that I wanted to be a global agri company. I could see myself as a 1,000 crore company in the next 15 years with a market cap of 20 million dollars. He further asked, 'What do you not want to do?' I said, 'I don't want to do any proprietary trading. I don't want to put up a plant, waste my time on processing and so on. I want to be a service provider.' Then he enquired, 'So what's the hurdle?' I said, 'We're just a start-up, we're providing good services but it's been only three years. I need to operate from Mumbai, right now we're in Jaipur. From Jaipur I can't see the whole of India. From Mumbai I can.'"

After the patient hearing he gave Amith and his partners, Ramesh Chandra's words of wisdom were wrapped up and imparted in an unforgettable way.

"He told us an interesting story," recalled Amith. "He said that in the board room he had once asked his sons what their dreams were. They had big aims, to keep growing and touch the sky. It was like achieving heaven. What he told them was what he repeated to us: 'To achieve heaven you have to be prepared to die.' In short, to achieve such big goals, you had to put your life into it, give it complete commitment. It's like you're in Siachen, it doesn't matter whether it's minus 45 degrees or minus 60. You have to move towards your goal, your *lakshya*. If you have that much ambition to grow and achieve so much, you must be prepared to die for it."

But Ramesh Chandra was not an elder who only dispensed verbal wisdom, he was a man who would get down to brass tacks and supply practical help too.

Like the time he asked Amith, 'What do you want in Mumbai?' And Amith answered, 'We want an office.' To the young man's surprise, the next time they met in Mumbai, Ramesh Chandra sent them to check out an office but said, 'I won't give it to you for free. What I can give you is flexibility in payment.'

"That was his lesson to us," Amith recalled. "He said to us, 'Don't take it amiss but if it's free, it'll be like social service and you won't be serious about your business. If you've got an expense on your head, you'll run faster to pay it.'"

Amith and his partners looked up to him for guidance and

he gave them his most valuable commodities—his time and his wisdom. "He would say, strategise, plan, review. We didn't have a review mechanism in place. So he advised, 'Every Monday morning at 9 am you should have a review meeting.' He said that he had also made a lot of mistakes at the start of his career and wanted us to learn and benefit from his experience. He had nothing to gain from us."

For the man who'd hit a goldmine with DB and allied businesses, mentoring enthused youngsters like Amith was like another project where he invested his time, expertise and acuity, drawing satisfaction from their success and growth.

When investors showed an interest in StarAgri, Ramesh Chandra told his proteges to first set up a good Board of Directors and was impressed when they got a former RBI Executive Director and a former Planning Commission Chairman, eminent men on board. "We invited Mr Agarwal to also join our board but he declined saying, 'I don't want any financial, monetary benefit. I just want to be your advisor. My blessings are with you.' He was giving me everything like he would to a son. That was the feeling I got from him, it's difficult to put it into words.

"Always smiling, always cheerful, when we'd go to meet him, he'd greet us as if Ratan Tata had come into the room. He gave that much respect to a person. He just made you feel so good.

"When he set up the plant in Kota, he even mentioned us in his speech and said, 'I will put this up for these boys. They'll run it, they'll do the procurement.' It just made you feel so special.

"Rameshji was a huge Hanuman *bhakt*," Amith noted. "He would use the Hanuman analogy in business. He'd talk of his loyalty, his strength in carrying the mountain, his tireless work. He'd link Hanuman to business, relate characteristics of the Monkey God to business, commitment, loyalty. The *kabhi na thaknewala*, the untiring attitude came to him from Hanumanji."

Akhilesh Rathi of Indore who looked after the textiles business of the DB Group, flew to Mumbai to give inputs on his closest friend and business associate. Sitting in a five-star coffee shop, he wept unabashedly as he spoke.

"People knew him socially, professionally, commercially, as a family or as a friend but I knew each of these dimensions of his life. I was involved with him on all these fronts and more," said Akhilesh in his tribute to the dear departed. "That's why I get very upset when I talk about him."

Although he had first met Ramesh Chandra very briefly in 1985 when he was a trainee with the finance consulting firm Sethi & Associates in Indore, Akhilesh came into closer contact with him around 1995 when the *Bhaskar* Chairman required inputs in merchant banking for a project.

"It started off as a professional relationship but gradually became personal, familial and social. No relationship can mature in a day, it takes its natural time but it happened continuously. He was senior to me by 23 years but he loved me, inspired me to think big, take larger risks and be more enterprising. However, he also cautioned me that one should take risks in such a way that one does not sink.

"For instance, in 2007, when we went into a partnership, he gave me two golden rules to follow: he advised me to invest in it but also said, 'Take care that even if you're looking at gold, you invest only to the extent where even if there's a reversal, you won't break out into a sweat.' So while he was aggressive, he was also balanced."

It was in 2008 that their strongest and longest surviving partnership took off when Ramesh Chandra entrusted the man from Indore with the running of his textile wing—a business understanding that continued with Akhilesh meeting Pawan once a month for detailed updates.

Rathi learnt and shared a range of wise thoughts that he had collected from the man who thrived on relationships.

"He was also a man who said, it's necessary to have scorpions and snakes too around you," Rathi revealed, "because sometimes, there are certain jobs that only these creatures can get done for you. So they too have their uses. But you should be judicious and know how much distance to keep from them. They should be far enough not to harm you but not so far that they can't do your work for you.

"Rameshji was my business-father. He taught me enterprise, risk-taking, building on ideas, taking risks on ideas, investing in people. He strengthened me in all those areas and concepts. He also said, 'Always listen to your inner voice.' He believed that there were solutions to all problems and all you had to do was to connect your antenna to that solution.

"We talked every day for at least half-an-hour. His life revolved around learning, teaching and sharing. He also believed that there should be a chain impacting others. You must help improve the quality of life around you."

Rathi had some great learning experiences from Ramesh Chandra, one of which involved a 150-year-old *gaushala* (shelter for cows). "Initially, each cow there was fed Rs 7 worth of grass. When he got involved, Rameshji enquired, 'What's the right nutritional feed for cows?'A friend from America who had knowledge about this said, 'Rs 22 per kilo would give the best feed for cows.' Rameshji insisted that health care, hygiene and nutrition should be world class, the cows should get the best. He asked everybody to budget it and decide the loss for the first year; he was ready to bear more than 50 per cent of the loss. He said, 'Take more money if you want but there should be no compromise on what's fed to the cows. If you do *seva,* service, do it unstintingly.'

"He got us to make systems, improve processes, stop leakages, look at improving the quality of food and the output quality, and to factor in the value additions of by-products like *gobar* (fertiliser from the dung) and *gau mutra* (cow urine, said to be efficacious, to have medical properties), and to make it self-sufficient in two years."

A far bigger *gaushala* that was spread over 100 acres in Indore underwent a complete transformation once Ramesh Chandra touched it with his wand.

"With the systems he set in place, both *gaushalas* are now top-of-the-line," came Rathi's approbation. "Every cow is tagged, there's Management Information System (MIS) of every little detail. This is just one example of how he operated. There were countless such projects that he took on and turned.

"After launching his paper everywhere and concentrating on his media business, at the age of 50, he turned to manufacturing. Then wondered, why limit himself to Rs 100 and 200 crore investment and he turned to the power industry. He studied a 100-megawatt project, then aero engines and finally decided that a one billion-dollar, 1,200-megawatt set-up would be the most viable one: thermal-based, coal-based, a dream project. He knew that they didn't have the experience out here. But he had great faith that his sons and his team would show tremendous capability in executing any project. With that confidence he went into it. He went into so many enterprises, some failed, others steamed ahead. But he was an entrepreneur *non pareil*.

"Other people were setting up power plants with Chinese technology. He and his sons studied it minutely and selected BHEL as the best for equipment with L&T for execution, instead of Chinese. They didn't believe in going for smaller options, they went for top quality. Like him, there's extraordinary fire power in his sons too."

Ramesh Chandra would also advise Rathi to learn when to step back.

"One learnt from him how much to be involved and when to withdraw. He had that extraordinary ability to withdraw and hand things over to others. He would say, 'Put your house in order and watch from a distance. If you are the eternal doer, you will never be able to observe from a distance.' He had great clarity on this.

"He was however, a poor reader. His knowledge came from talking and listening. He thoroughly enjoyed his people-connect and he didn't network for business alone, he also networked for expanding his knowledge. He was well-informed with a sound grip on current and economic affairs because of his quest for knowledge. He won over people with his utter simplicity and immense knowledge. People usually meet a man for his power and position. But in Rameshji's case, people loved connecting with him, they'd come away feeling elevated. He was a rare and complete man."

Many toil, many succeed. But not many leave behind such a rich legacy.

Many are the sayings that are a perfect fit for Ramesh Chandra Agarwal.

'Do a little more each day than you think you possibly can,' said American writer, actor, broadcaster and traveller, Lowell Thomas.

Ramesh Chandra did a little more every day until the last step of his life.

Bhaskar signified brilliance, illumination like the Sun, the Creator.

Ramesh was another name for Lord Vishnu, The Preserver.

He steered *Dainik Bhaskar* to live up to its name of brilliance.

He himself lived up to his name and preserved all that was precious for mankind.

He symbolised
Success does not have to breed arrogance
There's strength in unity, in family
Networking and people skills are paramount

Be a student all your life
Nurture talent around you, let others flower and blossom too
Give back, give back, give back to society. It's important for the soul.
Important for immortality.
Ramesh Chandra Agarwal didn't really bid adieu on 12 April 2017.

Chapter 9

THE BHASKAR PARIVAAR

'What is most important almost always involves the people around us'

–Thomas S Monson

The people around Ramesh Chandra were those who grew alongside DB and nurtured it from the inside. They mattered. They grieved too but only for the emptiness wrought by his physical absence. In every other way, DB itself lived on, standing sturdy on the unshakeable foundation he had laid in his lifetime. The people were his bricks. He built pillars with them, invested in them, placed trust in them, and stood watching them take over with the efficiency he had inculcated in each one of them.

As one of the bureaucrats observed, 'There's no earthquake out there at DB.' A strong indicator of its healthy functioning after the demise of its omniscient Chairman was that there was no sweeping change made at the workplace, no pink slips given overnight, no sense of insecurity prevailing at any level.

In fact, the 4th son syndrome surfaced when Senior Vice-President Vinay Maheshwari spoke of his personal equation with him.

"When he took his last breath, I would've been the only person standing next to him because we were to fly down together. But he went to Delhi and said, 'I'll meet you in Ahmedabad.' We'd flown that morning Indigo flight from Delhi to Ahmedabad together many times. He had told me, 'No need to come to the airport, I'll meet you at the office.' So I was at the office when I heard from Sudhirji what had happened at the airport and rushed to the hospital. By the time I reached, he had collapsed, the doctors were trying to revive him. I was there all through. When the doctor said, 'He has taken his last breath,' I instantly read out the Hanuman Chalisa. I can never forget that moment. I had tears in my eyes.

"I can't explain the feeling. All I can say is, it was a huge personal loss for me. The way he treated me, it was like I was his fourth son. I always felt that way. The feeling I got from him was that I was no different from his three sons.

"My wife and he shared the same birthday, 30 November. When I would call him to wish him, he would say, '*Hema ko bhi wish karna* (wish Hema too from me).' He would always remember. Those were his personal touches.

"When we initiated the Gujarat project, he called me up and said, 'I met Morari Bapu who gave me something.' It was Rameshji's belief and he shared that with me. That paper is still with me," said Vinay. "Morari Bapu had given him something, told him to travel in all four directions of Gujarat and scatter it. Rameshji could have given this task to any of his sons but he wanted me to carry it out for him."

As long as Vinay was with DB, although he reported to Sudhir, "It was a different kind of relationship with Rameshji.

If he was in Bhopal, he would definitely call me between 8.30 and 9 in the morning. The only thing he would ask was, '*Aur Vinay, kya chal raha hai*?' That was his trademark line which I can hear to this day. He would then expect me to share with him what was happening around the world, what was happening with me, with the circulation department. It would eventually come to a point where I would say, 'Okay, I'll come at 5 pm.' Whenever he was in Bhopal and I was also there, we would meet at 5 pm. He was very particular about being punctual. He carried no pen or paper with him but his secretary would call at 10 minutes to 5 and say, 'Are you reaching? You've an appointment with Sir at 5.'

"The last one year before he passed away, I worked very closely with him. We travelled a lot on chartered and commercial flights, had long, long meetings that would start at 7.30 am and finish at 11 pm. When I would ask him why he was taking so much stress, he would say, 'There's no stress when you love your job.'

"I remember the day he called me and said, 'I have picked up this Gujarat project, will you work with me?' And I said, 'Any day, Sir.' I really learnt a lot from him. I've worked with a lot of promoters and professionals. There's a conscious learning and there's a subconscious one. There's doctrine learning and structural learning. With him, it was everything. He had great conviction and belief in what he did. He was extremely clear about what could happen and what could not.

"We have his photograph in all board rooms and offices. To this day, I always first offer prayers to him before his photograph and then start work. From his smiling face, I still get a message. I talk to him. When I have my meetings with my team, at times I feel he's nodding. He's in my thoughts all the time. All that I learnt from him is far more valuable than anything else that I have learnt in my life."

Group Executive Director Dr Bharat Agarwal turned the spotlight on Ramesh Chandra's outstanding capacity to take heart-stopping risks.

"The one important factor behind the entire business, from building it from scratch to what it is today, was his supreme risk-taking capacity. He used to always tell me that every time he earned Rs 5 crore, he would plan a project of the same amount. He'd invest his last year's profit in expansion or a new business. He often told me, 'When I used to earn Rs 8 crore, I would do a new business with that amount. Now my sons, they earn a profit of Rs 400 crore but don't take the risk of even Rs 50 crore.' In their place, he would have done another 500 crore business. He always said, '*Yaar*, my sons are so conservative, they don't take risks.'"

What gave Bharat consolation was that the man who picked him from the world of medicine and plonked him in the political and business arena, walked away when he was in his element.

"The last six months of his life were most exciting," he recalled with contentment. "I can use a medical word and say that the business was like an aphrodisiac for him. Since he was hands-on in Gujarat, it was a stimulant for him. He was fully charged, fully active and was actually feeling like a young man.

"Oh, he slept soundly too. He would have a post-lunch nap come what may. And he would sleep soundly at night after watching a movie on television.

"So death came by chance. None of us were prepared for it."

A chartered accountant who gave up his practice in Indore and tested corporate waters in 1994 was DB stalwart Pradyumna Gopalkrishna Mishra, the Group CFO. How Ramesh Chandra initiated him into his world told a story of pragmatism laced with human understanding.

"A friend of mine asked me to meet Rameshji for an interview," remembered PG Mishra. "I met him for about half an hour, then Sudhirji for about 15 minutes. A week later he called me and said, 'Mishraji (that's what he called me), you're taking a very big decision in your life. Come to Bhopal for six days and look at our system of working.'" DB was still to take off in a big way and inviting Mishraji to test the waters before taking the big leap, accented the thoughtfulness of the newspaper proprietor who accorded due respect to a senior CA who was contemplating joining his company.

PGM soon realised, "Rameshji's grasp of a subject was so tremendous that 25 CAs in front of him would fail to match his knowledge and wisdom. He would ask for options within the ambit of the law; he always followed the law. I never ever heard him utter phrases like 'bend the rule'.

"I left my private practice at the right time for the right person," he said with satisfaction.

"I have done so much work with him, gone through so many accounts and balance sheets with him, I have learnt from him through it all. The most important quality he had was of not interfering in the field you were an expert at. He respected your knowledge and listened to you. His objective was: the work that you are here for, do it without interference in the best interests of the company."

He witnessed the Chairman's grounded earthiness again and again. "In 2011, we had gone to Indore for some bank work," he remembered. "I had already informed the bank that Rameshji was coming. We'd gone from Bhopal in a Lancer and when the manager asked him how come he didn't travel in a Mercedes, Rameshji answered, 'If there's a car that'll bring me from Bhopal to Indore half-an-hour earlier, I'll buy it. If it's only as a status symbol or to show off, I'm not interested.' *Bahut hi saral swabhav ke thay*. He was an extremely simple man."

DB did buy its own private plane, "But it was never a big deal for him, I've never heard him even mention it. A plane of

Rs 40-45 crore was a small thing for him," Mishra shrugged it away. "For him, it was, invest in your business first. These small little things didn't matter, it all boiled down to only convenience for him. His time was valuable. The connectivity from Bhopal was poor then and for him, getting a private plane was only a question of maximum utilisation of time."

Ravi Sawla, Vice-President, Real Estate, was confident that Ramesh Chandra's sons would take his legacy forward. "But he would take risks a little more than his sons do," he echoed Bharat Agarwal's words. "Like if we were doing an analysis of a business, Chairmansaab would say, 'As long as what we're putting in is covered, let's take the risk. Let's give it a try.'"

Ravi too joined in 1996 as an accountant but got challenges that went far beyond lifeless ledger-keeping. He started reporting to the Chairman once DB went into real estate which is spread over Indore, Gwalior and Ahmedabad, and talked of the ethics that the Chairman had set as a template for them to follow.

"Because we're a media house, the effort is to make sure we proceed with zero error in all permissions and rules," he said. "His approach was that we must follow rules and ensure that everything was 100 per cent above-board. If your reputation is affected then it will affect the reputation of the paper too and the whole family is keen on keeping its integrity intact."

On 12 April 2017, Ravi was travelling from Indore to Bhopal when a phone call stopped him in his tracks. Like Vinay, Ravi was a part of the core team that had worked with Ramesh Chandra on rejuvenating DB in Gujarat.

"He had *bhayankar,* awesome energy," said Ravi. "Just recently, we were working in Raipur with a consultant who had come from Gujarat and had been on his feet from 5 am. We worked till midnight when the Chairman said, 'We will meet again at 6 am.' I suggested, 'Let's meet at 9 am, people have come from elsewhere.' And he said, 'You're young, you should be saying 4 am when I say 6 am.' He had that kind of energy.

"I wish I'd worked for another 10 years with him, I'd have done my PhD in Business," he said volubly. "With Sudhirji I could do my post-grad, with him it would've been a PhD. Both of them have such a clear vision."

Ramesh Chandra had made a fine art out of gathering a family-like team around him, a home team that played best under his captaincy.

Sawla revealed how Ramesh Chandra's mind worked. "Chairmansaab had a different way of thinking," he stated. "When I'd say, 'Why didn't I think of it like you did?' he'd say, 'Give it a lot of thought. Then keep it aside, give it a rest and think deeply about it again. You'll always find a different way of doing it.'"

It was his sheer energy that rejuvenated those who worked closely with him. After 21 years of working with DB, Sanjay Jain, Vice President—DB Malls & Hotel Business, missed the boss who kept them on their toes.

"There's no life without challenges," he smiled as he recalled the crazy schedules they kept where even before one assignment ended, the Chairman had another one ready for him.

"During the launch of the Jaipur radio station, I got a message that Chairmansaab wanted to talk to me. I thought he would have something to say about how to improve the radio station, etc. But he called me and said, 'We've bought 6 acres of land at an auction in Bhopal. We want to build a mall there. Wind up here, hand it over to a team, come to Bhopal and start the mall work. It's a large piece of land, nothing like what we have in mind has been made in Bhopal before. Study it, and we'll construct it.'"

The excitement was thus a constant as Jain didn't get time to blink as he moved from newspaper to radio to real estate. It hardly occurred to him that he'd actually started life as a Chartered Accountant.

Emotions surfaced when National Editor—Mobile App—

Navneet Gurjar went into depression after the death of the Chairman.

The hardened editor wept as he talked—he hadn't got over the loss or come to terms with it entirely. Within six months of his Chairman's death, Navneet had packed his bags from Gujarat and returned to Bhopal.

"I did take Chairmansaab's death very personally," he admitted. He had stood vigil from 11 am to 4 pm at the hospital in Ahmedabad, perhaps expecting a miracle to happen.

"It was a strange experience," he remarked. "We were actually waiting for him to chair a meeting at the office. We'd kept a pile of reports this high ready for him. I was still at the guest house and running a bit late when I called up Anil Gupta, his PA. He told me that Chairmansaab has gone directly to the hospital from the airport. I breathed a sigh of relief and thought, okay, *chalo*, I've got half an hour more to reach office. But after 10 to 15 minutes, I called up Hemant and asked him why the Chairman had gone straight to hospital. All he told me was, 'Just come over to the hospital'.

"On the way itself, I got to know what had happened. I was there all through but there was no question of him taking his last breath there. They tried reviving him for over an hour but no, there was really no revival." The end had come at the airport itself.

His voice broke with emotion when he referred to Ramesh Chandra's wonderful quality of coming down to the level of the other person and communicating like a friend, without ever coming across as patronising. Otherwise, he would've never touched so many hearts with so much warmth. "There was never ever any show that he was the boss."

The balancing act of business, PR and editorial freedom, most times horribly tilted one way or the other by many a publisher, was what Ramesh Chandra had perfected.

"He was simple and practical and also very fearless, *dabbang*," said his editor. "Once, a very senior political leader, one who was right up there in the hierarchy of the ruling party, came to meet him after 8 pm to complain that the paper was regularly publishing stories against him. The Chairman heard him for about half an hour, then sent for me. We spoke for a while and then I went to see the visitor to the lift. When I returned, the Chairman told me, 'He had a lot of complaints against you.' I replied, 'If we write against him, he's bound to.' Rameshji's response was, 'There should be complaints. It means you're writing *nishpaksh*, without taking sides. The day people stop complaining, we'll be finished. If there are no complaints, I would myself be suspicious that we write only goody-goody stuff.' He was that kind of boss. Where do you find such proprietors today?" asked the veteran journalist.

Although Navneet was the State Editor of DB, his Chairman's sources were even more impeccable than his. "Politically, he had his ear to the ground, he knew what was going on. He had so many contacts everywhere. He would give us many story ideas, pass on many stories to us. He would never care for politicians and ministers."

He goaded his team to go out and network. He would tell editors, 'Go out and meet people, meet two, three people every day, stay connected with them. Don't meet them as editors, meet as individuals, as common people.'

'The art of being wise is the art of knowing what to overlook,' said American philosopher and psychologist, William James. Ramesh Chandra had the knack of investing in the right people precisely because he looked at their strengths, not at their weaknesses. The loyalty he earned in return was exemplified in men like Managing Editor, Jagdish Sharma.

Displaying frankness without inhibition, he unstintingly acknowledged the role DB had played in his life.

"I came from a lower middle-class family and would travel around on a scooter. At that time, I didn't even have friends who had a car. The first time I sat in one was with DB. So it goes without saying that the first time I flew in a plane was also with DB. I bought my first car, a Maruti 800 because of DB. My first personal Mercedes also came from DB," Sharma said, as he discussed the DB culture.

"In DB, you don't get in through recommendations, through flattery. You make it in this group solely because of what you can do. I have been here for 23 years. I have never been fluent in English," he offered as an example. "But in DB, I was never made to feel it was a shortcoming. I have held every possible post in the group, have worked in every department (not just editorial) and that was possible because here they only look at a person's worth, they don't look at his shortcomings." The art of knowing what to overlook.

Outlining the editorial freedom of the team, he said, "It was clear that you couldn't use the paper to attack a *dushman* (enemy). Nor could you use the paper to promote a *dost* (friend)."

An unforgettable journalistic nugget he remembered dated back to, "Bhairon Singh's government in Rajasthan which troubled us as much as any *sarkaar* could trouble a paper. As long as he was in power, the state wouldn't give any advertisements to DB. But we continued writing fearlessly. Once, a crime reporter wrote a story about the police losing a wireless set because they were drunk. To suppress DB, the government decided to arrest the reporter. Rameshji called the reporter and said, 'You don't have to fear anything. You shift to MP, this government cannot arrest you there.' He gave his team that kind of support. If a reporter made a mistake, he never asked him to leave the company. He would say, 'Give me the facts behind the story and if you're right, I'll fight the world on your behalf. And if you're wrong, tell me, and I'll say 'sorry' on your behalf.'"

Yet another fourth son appeared on the scene when Jagdish remarked, "In all the 22 years that I have been here, he never ever made me feel that I work in this company. His sons follow the same tradition. But I'll always feel his *kami,* his absence personally. I always called him 'Papaji', never Chairmansaab. Whenever anything happened, any little success, anything at all, I would call up Papaji first. I miss that."

After 22 years of being a member of the frenzied team that pulled off impossible deadlines at various launches of DB, CTO RD Bhatnagar watched his Chairman succeed practically on every front, especially when it came to people.

"When I say he was simple, it was not about his attire or the way he talked. He was the most accessible person in the company till the last day of his life. He would stand and watch people, look at their facial expressions, look at their body language and understand what was needed. He knew the nerve of each and every stake holder in the newspaper.

"His three sons have been very hardworking but I don't think the kind of vision that Chairman Sir had, has been passed down to them yet. It will take its own time because they are also in the same state as we are. It must be difficult for them to also come around to accepting that he's no more because nobody expected this to happen," RD analysed.

"I remember him saying, 'I told my sons, you go after the crops while I believe in planting trees.'"

On 12 April 2017, when the illustrious son of Bhopal slumped on the last step of the elevator at Ahmedabad airport, an autopsy was not required to certify that his body contained large amounts of a quartet of hormones.

Endorphins, the positive well-being hormone released by a daily constitutional or any physical exercise.

Dopamine, released by the pleasure of materialistic acquisition that comes with success.

Serotonin, the warm hormone that suffuses the body after acts that benefit others.

And Oxytocin, the social hormone that a network of friends and family alone can release in the body.

In a span of 72 well-lived years, it came effortlessly to Ramesh Chandra Agarwal to pack his insides with the Foursome of Happiness.

In his wisdom, he left behind a legacy that was put in place well within his lifetime; an empire that he handed his three sons, experiencing the rare pleasure of watching them take the baton and sprint together in natural rhythm. He also bid adieu with bonds so strong that two more generations of family members held hands on all occasions happy and sad, to function seamlessly as one.

Inside the bungalow that Ramesh Chandra built in Bhopal much to the envy of many, and inside the staggering edifice that housed the legendary *Dainik Bhaskar*, a visible mark of respect encapsulated the sentiments.

His room at home remained as it always was, like he was still its valued occupant. The large Chairman's room in the bustling Bhaskar Bhavan too stayed untouched. His smiling face all over every DB office.

Sudhir Agarwal is the Managing Director of the DB group.

Girish Agarwaal, Director.

Pawan Agarwal, Director.

On paper there may be another Chairman tomorrow.

But the Chairman in the hearts of people will only be Ramesh Chandra Agarwal.